Honor Your Parent

By

Dr. Randall Kinnison
with
Mark Duhrkoop
Kim Christensen

HONOR YOUR PARENT
Copyright © 2023

All rights reserved. No part of the publication may be reproduced, stored in retrieval systems, or transmitted in any form or by any means electronic, mechanical, photocopy, recording, or any other except for brief quotations in printed reviews, without the prior permission of the publisher.

Scripture quotations are taken from the Holy Bible, English Standard Version, The ESV® Bible. ESV® Permanent Text Edition (2016). Copyright © 2001 by Crossway, a publishing ministry of Good News Publishers. Used by permission. All rights reserved.

Some names and identifying details have been changed to protect the privacy of individuals. Names, characters, businesses, places, events, and incidents are either the products of the author's imagination or used in a fictitious manner. Any resemblance to actual persons, living or dead, or actual events is purely coincidental.

Cover Design by Kentin Hosley
Technical Design by Kentin Hosley

Graphics by Dan Duhrkoop
Published by Genesis Publishing

ISBN 978-0-9998498-1-1

Printed in the United States of America
10 9 8 7 6 5 4 3 2 1

Dedication

This book is dedicated to Mark Duhrkoop, one of the authors. He was a major contributor to the book and a wonderful team member. Shortly after the release of The Decision Tree of Aging, the predecessor of Honor Your Parent, Mark suffered a major stroke and passed on November 26, 2021. A portion of the book sales are dedicated to Annie, his widow.

In addition, this book is dedicated to those who currently care for their parents. You are our heroes! If this book can help guide you in all the decisions and needs of how to Honor Your Parents, we will have succeeded!

Table of Contents

Dedication — 3
Acknowledgments — 7
About The Authors — 9
Start Here — 11

Part One: A Tale of Peace and Chaos

Chapter 1: The Decision Tree and the Choices We Make — 17
Chapter 2: Seedlings — 21
Chapter 3: New Growth on the Tree — 27
Chapter 4: Fruit and Harvest — 33
Chapter 5: Fall Leaves — 39
Chapter 6: Winter and Barren Branches — 47
Chapter 7: The Last Leaf on the Tree — 57

Part Two: The Honor Your Parent Process

Chapter 8: Root 1 - Wills and Estates — 67
Chapter 9: Root 2 - Income Streams and Assets — 75
Chapter 10: Root 3 - End-of-Life Plans — 83
Chapter 11: Root 4 - Support Plans — 91
Chapter 12: Branch 1 - How Will You Transition? — 95
Chapter 13: Branch 2 - When Will You Receive Care? — 99
Chapter 14: Branch 3 - Who Should Give The Care? — 103
Chapter 15: Branch 4 - Where Will You Receive Care? — 107

Epilogue — 113

Appendix

Example of the Decision Tree Plan — 117
Drop Dead File Checklist — 124
Example of Drop Deal File By Age Progression — 126
Examples of an Obituary — 132
Assessment Tools for Need of Care — 133
Cost of Aging in Home Versus Care Community — 135
Health Insurance For Seniors Over 65 — 137

Appendix (continued)

What To Do When Someone Dies   138
Helpful Resources   140

Acknowledgments

The major contents of Honor Your Parents was published as The Decision Tree of Aging in 2018. I want to acknowledge my original team from Genesis. Mark Duhrhoop, then the Executive Director of Genesis Life Transitions, and Kim Christensen, collaborated with me on the book. Mark and Kim both helped with copy, and Kim was instrumental in the research, editing, and compiling.

About The Authors

Randy's Story

As a pastor for 40 years, I saw the damage that can happen when families do not prepare for the inevitable. For the last fifteen years I have helped families find peace in a multitude of settings, including the aging process and end-of-life decisions. One of the most loving things you will do for your family in life is prepare for death. We all know our birthday. None of us know our death day. After years of witnessing the conflict and damage, I decided to do something about it. At first, Honor Your Parent was an instructional presentation I developed, but people were always requesting a book after I spoke. This book is written in the form of a parable to illustrate the peace or chaos created by our choices as we age. I hope that this book will help create peace for families and professionals by enabling educated choices and plans to mitigate future conflict.

Mark's Story

My brothers and I tried our best to take care of the various needs of our parents. At times, it took all of us and our spouses to do that. We thought we were meeting their needs. In reality, we made plenty of mistakes that caused use to lose precious time with our parents. As the end of life came for my parents, I began work with Dr. Kinnison on this book. We learned from our mistakes and our poor choices. When you can plan for success in the aging process, you reap the priceless rewards of peace and quality time.

Kim's Story

Honor Your Parent material was presented to me at a time when most of my friends were dealing with aging parents. I was also dealing with helping an adult daughter navigate the waters of being independent while struggling with a mental illness. Building relationships and helping others find meaningful purpose in life is something I enjoy. The idea of creating a book that would be available to help others navigate these same waters, and give them some control over their lives, was appealing. My hope is this book will save you from being thrown off balance when life throws you a curve ball.

Start Here

As a young boy, I enjoyed books with alternate endings, where I could choose the way the story would end. This project is about helping you choose your ending, your story. Honor Your Parent is a tale of two fictional families: Richard and Mary Jones, and James and Joy Smith. Richard and James grew up on the same block in Corvallis, Oregon. And although both boys grew up in similar fashion on their block, they ended up in very different places. Richard never thought about planning and decisions for death. James spent his whole life preparing and understanding the certainty of death. Both families grieved the loss of a loved dad and husband. The lack of planning by Richard created untold chaos for his family, while the planning James did brought order and peace. You are writing your own story, and just like the books where I could select the ending as a young boy, you get to select your ending. You get to write the way you want to live as well as the way you want to die. We cannot choose when or how we die, but we can make choices about the process of dying and how we can help our families make the most difficult decisions in life and death.

Honor Your Parent is a system to help families through the complexities and challenges of aging or disability. I use the analogy of a tree. For any tree to flourish, a strong root system is necessary. For your family to flourish through the aging process, building a root system is critical. The roots include various income streams to sustain cash flow, legal documents to protect people and assets, professional and personal teams for guidance and support, and a clear end-of-life plan to avoid conflict and confusion. When a strong root system exists, the leaves on the branches are healthy and strong. The branches are the forks in the road for major decisions through the aging process such as who will give care, when care will be given, where care will be received, and what thresholds will be that trigger transitions along the way. Honor Your Parent creates a roadmap to navigate the landscape of aging. The goal is to avoid chaos and conflict, while creating peace and comfort.

As a pastor for 40 years, I saw both sudden, tragic death and expected, languishing death. I held the hands of widows with small children, and those who shared a lifetime with their spouses. Death is never easy, regardless of the situation. I have seen the best of families torn apart over estate disputes: fights over land, rights, vacation homes, and grandma's dresser. Sometimes the damage lasts a lifetime, leaving relationships estranged.

In the last fifteen years, I have helped families who were at war find peace. Now, as a mediator, I work with the most difficult of situations. So often I shake my head and think, "This could have been avoided!" The dynamics in some families are so dysfunctional, regardless of the best intentions and planning, and the result will remain bumpy. However, for millions of others, the aging process and end-of-life decisions could be more peaceful, and more honoring of their loved ones.

As a culture, we are obsessed with prolonging life and avoiding even the discussion of death. More than 65 percent of the population do not have a will or trust and die intestate. The legal, physical, and emotional carnage left behind can be devastating to families.

After years of witnessing the conflict and damage, I decided to do something about it by writing this book. It was written in the form of a parable to illustrate the peace or chaos created by choices as we age. I know this book will be helpful, but there is so much more needed than one book. Families need somewhere to turn at 3:00 a.m. in the hospital waiting room. They need a system, a comprehensive aid to guide them through the complexities of legal, health, financial, and family dynamics. That is what Honor Your Parent is. In addition to this book, we have many online resources for you to use, and our appendix is full of valuable information and examples.

This is my world. A world of conflicted families, attorneys, time wasted, and thousands of dollars spent needlessly due to poor or incomplete planning. You can make decisions related to the aging process and death or abdicate those decisions to others, forcing them to guess at your wishes. At Genesis Mediation and Honor Your Parent, we are committed to creating peace for a million people by 2030. My hope and prayer is this book and our project helps fulfill that vision.

Honor Your Parent is for all ages. Death comes to all ages at any moment. One of the most loving things you will do for your family in life is prepare for death. We all know our birthday. None of us know our death day.

INTRODUCTIONS

Richard and Mary Jones
Son: Rex and wife, Brenda
      Grandchildren: Faith, Joey, and Malcolm
Daughter: Becky and boyfriend, Gary
      Grandson: B.J.

James and Joy Smith
Son: Jay and wife, Sarah
      Grandchildren: Eric, George, and Amy
Daughter: Jillian and husband, Robert
      Grandchildren: Tyler and Melanie
Son: Jared and wife, Theresa
      Guardians: David and Mara

Part One
A Tale of Peace and Chaos

This first part of the book is a fictional account of two families. James and Joy Smith, who chose to implement the Honor Your Parent process and tools, and Richard and Mary Jones, who deferred any decisions for aging. Thus, this is a story about peace and chaos.

The characters are fictional. However, the situations are real. The authors have experienced many of the issues either personally, or through case work. The stories of the authors are woven throughout the book. Your story might be there too.

Chapter One
THE DECISION TREE AND THE CHOICES WE MAKE

We are our choices.
- Jean-Paul Sartre

Richard Jones went out for his usual early morning walk as the rest of the house began to wake up. His daughter Becky got her son, B.J., started with cereal for breakfast while his wife Mary put his lunch together. While B.J. ate, Becky went to prepare herself for the day. She had a lot on her plate this week, and needed to make sure she stayed on track. Being a single mom and living with her parents, time was precious. Hopefully she would be able to find time with Mom after B.J. went off to school. When she came into the kitchen, Mary was nowhere to be seen, and the teakettle had boiled over. Turning off the burner, Becky began to call out for her mom. Mary came through the back door with a handful of flowers. "Mom, you left the burner on!" exclaimed Becky.

"Oh, I must have forgot, the flowers were so pretty. I just had to go cut some for the table," responded Mary.

Richard had started to notice a few things with Mary. She seemed forgetful at times. It was small things at first, barely noticable. When there were more and more incidents, it was harder to ignore it. Becky had started to notice it too, but she did not think much about it. Mary missed appointments here and there, but she had been helping with B.J. a lot while Becky studied for her exams. She knew how easy it was to lose track of time while watching B.J.

Mary, on the other hand, knew that something was off, but did what she could to make up for it. Notes and lists were becoming her friend, though she had never needed them before. She grew more concerned when she picked B.J. up at school and it took her much longer to get there than she had expected. Some roadwork on her regular route had confused her, and going a different way got her turned around. She would keep this a secret between her and B.J. for now. Mary didn't know it yet, but she had crossed a threshold in the aging process.

Just then, the doorbell rang. Becky answered the door. Two police officers stood on the porch. Her dad, Richard Jones, had been walking in the nearby park when he had a massive heart attack. Her mom sank to the floor, time and space no longer making sense. This day would become the longest day of Becky's life, with a hundred things coming at her. She would wonder how a day could be filled with so much activity and yet go so horribly slow.

Becky called Rex, her brother, to let him know. Then, Becky and Mary rushed to the hospital. Rex and his wife, Brenda, made it to the hospital just shortly after Mary and Becky arrived. They held hands in the waiting room, hoping for the best. Instead, the ER doctor came out and told them Richard did not make it. They sat there stunned. How had this happened? He had been so fit, so active all his life. In a moment, he was gone. Mary was numb and felt paralyzed. Then, the question came from the nurse. "Do you have any plans for the body?"

Mary had no idea. She turned to Becky. "What should we do?"

Mary decided to call a funeral home where she had recently attended a funeral. She had no idea of the costs or process. She just needed to make this one decision right now. Mary was unaware of the barrage of questions and decisions that would need to be made the next few days, let alone the months, to follow. After the nurse left, Mary sobbed uncontrollably. Her children just held her. Mary felt alone, scared, and anxious. Most of all, she just felt numb. Eventually, she gathered herself and told the kids, "Let's go home."

As they all entered the house, it felt eerily empty. Richard always had the TV or music on. He was such a gregarious and extroverted person. He loved to feel as if people were around him, even if alone.

It was a difficult night as they tried to figure out what to do. There were no funeral plans, and as a matter of fact there were no plans of any kind. There was so much to process. At one point, it sounded like Mary started to ask when Richard would be home, but she corrected herself. Becky pointed it out to Rex, who was sure it was just the stress of everything. Becky wasn't so sure. Becky helped Mary make phone calls, lots of them. They had to call family, they had to set up a meeting with the funeral home, the list went on and on. Rex and his wife, Brenda decided to go home. Everyone was exhausted and in shock.

"I'm glad you're here to help Mom." Rex said to his sister as they walked to the car. Rex exclaimed, "I wished Dad would have helped us be more prepared for this." They had no idea what lay ahead. Rex and Becky were left very unprepared and had to try and create order out of chaos. Becky turned and saw her mom, who suddenly looked a lot older to her. She took a big breath and headed back into the house.

Funeral planning can greatly assist your loved ones in their most difficult time.

ROOT: End of Life Plan.

Chapter Two
SEEDLINGS

Nature herself does not distinguish between what seed it receives. It grows whatever seed is planted; this is the way life works. Be mindful of the seeds you plant today, as they will become the crop you harvest.
- Mary Morrissey

Richard Jones realized early in his career that sales were natural for him. As a kid, he could sell his neighbors anything for his soccer fundraisers growing up.

Richard won a soccer scholarship to Portland State with no idea what he wanted out of college other than a good time. The first semester was not too bad. He made passing grades without much work, cutting class most of the time. He focused on soccer. The next semester classes became more difficult, and a few of his professors included attendance in their grading. Richard flunked most of his classes. He was put on academic probation and couldn't play soccer.

The next semester, he attended class and did some homework. He was reinstated and back to playing soccer. Just when he was becoming the star of the team and dreaming about professional soccer, he was injured. The ACL surgery meant a year in rehab. Between hating the classroom and a year to come back, he decided to drop out. That was enough for him. He was working part-time at a local auto sales lot. He was making good money without much work. College was boring, sales was fun. The economy was good, people were buying cars, and he was making more money than he ever dreamed of. He bought a new car, moved into a nice apartment, and was living large.

Richard began dating Mary, the administrative assistant at the dealership. He was always the fun-loving life of the party. Mary was more conservative but was drawn to Richard's gregarious personality. After dating for six months, Richard asked Mary to move in with him.

Mary truly loved him; Richard drew her out of her shell. Her only concern was even though Richard was making good money, he was always broke. He had nothing in savings. Mary made only a fourth of what Richard made, yet she had managed to create an emergency fund of a few thousand dollars. She didn't want to let Richard know about it. She was fearful it would quickly be spent just like the rest of his money. After moving in, they often needed Mary's income to pay rent. She never knew where all the money went. After paying the rent, Mary would put the rest away in savings. She liked knowing a safety net was there.

The dealership provided Richard and Mary with a small life insurance policy. They both listed each other as beneficiaries. They never talked about what might happen if either one of them was in a serious accident, or even died. Mary tried to bring up the topic every once in a while. Richard was very uncomfortable with the topic, so he either changed the subject, made a joke about it, or just ignored it. They didn't know what the other wanted if something tragic happened. This bothered Mary, but Richard not so much. He was too busy living life!

Richard knew James Smith. They grew up on the same block in Corvallis, OR. James was the middle child of George and Marilyn Smith. His dad was an engineer, and with Oregon State University just minutes away from the house, he was destined to follow in his father's steps. James graduated with honors from high school and began his degree in mechanical engineering at OSU.

George wanted to help James think about the future now that he was 18. He took James aside for a "father-son" talk, and introduced him to Honor Your Parent concept of the Decision Tree. Together, they looked up what decisions are needed as a young adult. James was surprised to discover he needed a "Drop Dead File." He was just 18. He had no plans to die anytime soon!

Drop Dead File: A checklist of items and your decisions/papers that provide the information your family needs to ensure your plans are in place for your death and funeral. See Appendix.

His father told James a story about a college friend of his, Larry. Larry was out at a party one night during college. He had too much to drink and made the decision to drive home. He never made it. Instead, his car went off the road and hit a tree. Larry did not die immediately. He suffered severe injuries that left him in a coma with only minimal brain activity. His parents were faced with the painful decision to keep his body alive or pull the plug on the ventilator. After six months of lost hope and consultations with neurologists, they made the difficult decision to pull the plug. Larry died within an hour. His parents fought over what to do with his body. They really wanted a full funeral and burial, but things were tight with trying to put Larry through school. They were on the hook for his school loans as well. They ended up cremating the body with a simple service. They had no idea of how much time it took to sort out the medical bills. It took them years to repay the school loans.

James never dreamed how difficult even an untimely death as a young adult could cause so much time and effort for his parents. He got out the Drop Dead File Checklist. He walked through the items and checked them off one by one. Passwords to everything: check. It made him think about everything on his phone and computer. Would he want his parents to see his digital life? Just the thought of it helped him make a few decisions about the sites he visited, photos posted, and texts sent. A health directive: check. He felt weird checking boxes on the form if he wanted any heroics to save him or even tube feeding. He definitely wanted quality of life, not quantity. He realized his decisions would help his parents make difficult decisions easier. Life insurance: check. James secured a small policy to cover any student loans that might be accumulated. His parents were on the loans with him. He did not want them to carry a loan when, for a very small premium, he could alleviate that burden. Personal property: check. He made a short list of his cherished personal property informing his parents of the destination of each item. Saving for retirement: check. Wow, that one seemed surreal. Saving for retirement before landing your first career job. His dad went on a financial site and showed him the savings calculator. If he just saved $200 a month until he reached 68, he would have more than $500,000 at a minimum 5% rate of return. That is crazy. He set a simple goal of saving 10%, giving 10%, and spending the rest. He did not make much as a pizza delivery guy, but he was surprised how the savings began to grow.

James was still a fun-loving college kid with plenty of exploits of parties and pranks, but he felt good about this anchor in life. He was already preparing for his death and making decisions that would be loving and helpful to those around him.

In his sophomore year, James met Joy at a retreat. She was smart, fun, easy to talk to, and beautiful. They began dating and things turned serious quickly. As they began exploring values and how to eventually live together, James shared with Joy his "Drop Dead File." At first, it bothered Joy to be thinking about so many things surrounding death. The more she reflected on it, she realized that putting together the "Drop Dead File" was one of the most loving things she could do for her parents. With the help of James, she began checking off all the boxes as well. They knew once they were married, they would need to update their files. Joy even began saving 10%, giving 10%, and living on the rest. She also took out a small life insurance policy to help her parents with student loans. James told her how good it would feel to complete the "Drop Dead File." Now, she understood for herself. Joy was ready for life because she was ready for death.

James and Joy were married shortly after graduation. James began his career as a mechanical engineer at a firm in Portland and Joy landed a job in a local school district as a first-grade teacher. Once settled into new careers and a new city, James and Joy pulled out their "Drop Dead Files." They kept the small life insurance policies to help with student loans listing the parents as beneficiaries. They would still be the ones on the hook because they signed the papers! They thought about how much life insurance to have on each other. Children were more than a few years off, but they were hoping to get a house soon. They thought a great goal could be paying off a house and leaving a spouse with a little extra. Each of their jobs included a small life insurance policy. That would be the "extra" amount. Then, they each secured a $250,000 policy. At their age, the policies were not very expensive.

James and Joy went on the Honor Your Parent website to check what is needed once married. They were surprised to realize a will is a good idea, along with a durable power of attorney for both financial and health. They found a great attorney that had a package deal of all three items for a very reasonable amount. They could think of other needed areas for the money but knew how important these documents become in a health crisis. After leaving the attorney's office with all the documents signed, their "Drop Dead Files" updated and completed, they felt adequately prepared for the future. It was a comfort for them. They shared much of the file with their parents. They did not want any conflict between parents and a new spouse in a hospital corridor. Their parents were impressed with their maturity and planning. Their planning would serve them well through the challenges of life they would end up facing.

Legal documents for end-of-life planning are critical for peace instead of chaos.

ROOT: Will and Estates.

26

Chapter Three
NEW GROWTH ON THE TREE

An authentic and genuine life grows like a sturdy tree.
And like a tree, it grows slowly. Every time you make a
different and better decision, it grows a little.
- Steve Goodier

Five years later, James and Joy welcomed Jay into their lives. They had managed to pay off their school loans, even while Joy got her Master's degree. She went up on the pay scale upon the completion of her Master's, plus she already had five years of working experience. Their dream of buying a house became a reality three years ago. They had lived very simply to pay off school loans and saved enough for a down payment on a home.

With the addition of a baby, James and Joy needed to update their "Drop Dead File." At this point, they had far more to consider than when they first married. They reviewed the Honor Your Parent Decision Tree concept. James and Joy needed to begin building a Decision Tree Plan that would take them into retirement and beyond. They were only 27, yet there was much to do.

First, they increased life insurance to one million for James and $500,000 for Joy. The amount would be sufficient to pay off the mortgage of an even larger home, plus leave educational funds for Jay and a cushion for Joy. In the event of Joy's death, James would need to supply daycare or a nanny. His job was demanding, so a nanny would more than likely be necessary. Because the school loans were paid, they dropped the policies for the loans. They still had small policies from employers for immediate death benefit needs like upgrading vehicles or house maintenance.

Next, they needed to name guardians for Jay and other children who may follow and update their will. They thought long and hard over that choice. Because no family members were considered, they asked some good friends, David and Mara. They told their friends not just about being guardians, but their "Drop Dead File," will and other provisions. With $1.5 million in life insurance and the smaller policies from work, the total was $1.6 million. They had about $50,000 in equity in the house, plus another $50,000 in their retirement accounts. James and Joy told them the Decision Tree Plan in the event of their untimely deaths. First, they could use the life insurance proceeds as well as the equity in the home to help them buy a larger house, if needed. The funds were for them to help make life easier with the addition of Jay, or possibly other children, in their lives. They could buy a new minivan, house, or whatever they needed.

Selecting the right people for the right positions on your support team is essential!

ROOT: Support Team

Then, the will instructed the Personal Representative, James' dad, to set up a trust with the life insurance and retirement funds. If James' dad was able, he would act as trustee. A local bank was in second position if James' dad was no longer able to fulfill the duties. David and Mara could use the interest on the principle to help with living expenses. The income would allow Mara to stay home with the children as an option.

Once Jay, or possibly other children, reached college age, they could access the trust for educational purposes. Upon their 25th birthdays, they would receive a small distribution, about $10,000. Then, upon their 30th birthdays, they would receive a larger distribution, about $50,000. James and Joy wished the first distribution would help with a car after graduation. However, they were a little leery about giving too much, too soon. They hoped the second distribution would be a down payment for a home. Finally, the last distribution at age 35 would be $100,000 if funds were available. The trustee could also grant up to $20,000 for weddings.

When David and Mara saw all the planning of James and Joy, it was much easier to say, "Yes!" David and Mara knew some friends who needed to serve as guardians for some family members. It was a nightmare. The state had to appoint them guardians. There was no money to help them. They went from a family with two kids to five kids without any more funds to help. They struggled at times not to feel frustrated or even angry at the parents.

David and Mara heard the frustration and financial pressure felt by their friends. They were cautious until they saw all the planning of James and Joy. David and Mara had a great deal of confidence of being able to fulfill their duties as guardians. In fact, David and Mara were so impressed, they began putting together their own "Drop Dead File."

James and Joy went on to have two more children: Jillian and

Jared. Everything they put in place for Jay was sufficient for Jillian and Jared as well. Time went on, and the children grew up.

When Jared, the youngest, turned 18, there was no longer any need for guardians. James's dad was showing some signs of slipping, so appointing someone else as Personal Representative and trustee was a good idea. James and Joy talked it over. They felt their oldest, Jay, could handle the obligations of Personal Representative and Trustee, especially with the help of their attorney, even though at that time he was only 25 and newly married.

James and Joy had continued to accumulate wealth and now needed to consider implementing a trust instead of a will, especially because they lived in Oregon where the inheritance tax threshold was so much lower than the federal. While Jillian and Jared were still in college, James and Joy kept the life insurance in place. However, the instructions for Jay shifted a little from when David and Mara were guardians. The smaller life insurance policies from work now rolled into the trust, as well as all their retirement funds. James and Joy had kept their first house as a rental when they purchased their current home. Between life insurance and other assets, their total net worth approached $2 million dollars. While they felt good about leaving each other with plenty of assets, in the unusual circumstance of them both dying together, they felt leaving the kids one million between the three of them was more than sufficient. They wanted to help their kids, not unintentionally enable them. They picked out a few of their favorite charities to divide the other million from the estate. James and Joy went to the attorney to make the changes and brought Jay.

James and Joy are now grandparents and entering a whole new phase of life. The kids all have developed families of their own. This new phase meant a whole different level of planning for the Decision Tree Plan

Trusts are important vehicles for tax and estate planning.

ROOT: Will and Estates.

Some parents want to hide their assets from their children for fear of what the kids may someday do to them. That was not their fear. They wanted Jay to have full knowledge of everything in the Decision Tree Plan. The attorney was a very important piece of that plan, and Jay needed to trust her. After reviewing everything, the attorney counseled them to begin thinking about moving from a will to a trust.

Richard and Mary had a little surprise after living together for a couple of years, a baby. When they realized Mary was pregnant, they decided to get married. Mary had talked Richard into allowing her to manage the money. That helped. Richard still spent freely, but at least Mary could control some of it. She had managed to save enough for a down payment on a small house. Mary was worried about a larger mortgage payment than rent, and she wanted to stay home with her kids. She worked out a budget, and if Richard could continue selling at his present pace, they could afford everything. The only problem was Richard needed to reel in his spending. That scared her. He promised to make the mortgage payment before any other spending. They welcomed baby Rex into the world in their tiny new home.

Richard and Mary wanted another child after Rex, so Becky came along five years later.

Richard grew weary of the constant pressure of selling cars. He searched and found a great job in sales for a national company. He thrived in the new job and eventually became sales manager. He got a good bump in pay, plus bonuses and stock options. Richard and Mary decided to upgrade their house. Mary was a little worried about the increased monthly responsibilities. They always made it, but the debt load was adding up: car payments, house payments, and the balance on the credit card slowly accumulating. She loved her new house and being home with the kids. She concentrated on her world and let Richard worry about the money. Mary wanted to draw up a will, especially to appoint guardians for Rex and Becky. Every time she brought up the subject, they fought. They could not agree on guardians. Both of their families were a mess; there was nobody to choose from in the family tree. They considered friends. They had plenty of friends: Richard was a walking party. Everyone liked Richard. When they took a closer look at the lifestyles of their friends, they could not agree on whom to consider for guardianship. The friends Richard wanted, Mary objected. The friends

Mary wanted, Richard didn't like. So, they never got around to it. From time to time, this made Mary very uncomfortable. A friend told her of a family where the parents died without an appointment of guardians. She described all the drama and issues of family fighting over the kids and estate. The legal costs were staggering. Richard and Mary didn't have a big estate, but she wanted Rex and Becky to benefit from their work, not attorneys. She brought up the subject again to Richard. All they did was fight about it. So, she dropped it again.

Their son, Rex, graduated from high school and attended Portland Community College for a couple of years before eventually graduating from Portland State University with a computer science degree. Rex met Brenda at Portland Community College his freshman year. Brenda was in the paralegal program. They dated for a couple of years. When Brenda graduated with an Associate's Degree, she got a full-time job at a legal firm. Rex had transferred to Portland State University to complete his computer science degree. He could pay cash for tuition by working summers and a part-time job at a local tech company. With Brenda's new job, and only two years left of college, they decided to get married. They had to take out a couple of small loans for Rex to finish college. Upon graduation, Rex was brought on full-time at the tech firm. He was making good money. Rex and Brenda thought it was a good time to begin their family. Faith was born later that year, followed by Joey and Malcolm. Brenda found a job where she could do her paralegal work from home. It was a great fit with a growing family.

Rex's sister, Becky, enjoyed numbers and was good at it. She began at Portland Community College as well to save money. Like her brother, she transferred to Portland State University to complete her degree in accounting. She started a job at a large accounting firm in downtown Portland where she met Gary. They were both getting some experience before studying for the CPA exam.

They were only together for a short time when Becky became pregnant. Becky was not sure what to do. Gary offered to get married. The shine had already faded from the relationship. She was not sure of anything; to keep the baby or get married. She had just moved into her own place a year ago. She talked to her mom. Richard and Mary encouraged her to keep the baby. Mary would help with childcare. Becky decided to keep the baby and say goodbye to Gary. She gave up her apartment and moved back in with her parents, Richard and Mary. Gary decided to leave the firm to not make things awkward. Becky welcomed B.J. into the world a few months later. After her maternity leave, she launched into work as a single mother. Gary helped a little with child support and took B.J. every other weekend. They went through mediation to work out support and visitation. The mediator helped them retain a positive relationship as parents.

One thing Becky never considered was a will. She felt in the event of her death, B.J. would simply go to her parents. She was talking to another single mom one day at coffee. The conversation turned to the story of a mutual friend who died in a car accident. The father was a meth addict. His life was a mess. Her parents had a long legal battle to win custody of their granddaughter because of the lack of a will. Becky went home and called Gary. They met for coffee and mutually decided on guardians for B.J. and created wills to reflect their decision. Becky slept better the night after the will was signed. Little did Becky know the challenges ahead of her because of the lack of planning of her parents.

Chapter Four
FRUIT AND HARVEST

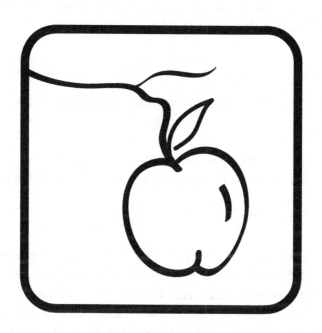

Two roads diverged in a wood, and I - I took the one less traveled by, And that has made all the difference.
- Robert Frost

James grew restless in middle age with engineering and decided to retire early and start his own auto speed shop. He always loved cars. The idea of working on fast cars to make them faster was like a dream come true. So at 58, he launched Smith's Speed Shop. He quickly became popular. His background of mechanical engineering and auto mechanics gave him a competitive edge in modifications. He was the "go-to guy" in the Portland area.

Jay followed in his father's footsteps of mechanical engineering after graduating from OSU. One day, James had a long talk with Jay about his job and future. Jay also loved cars. Smith's Speed Shop was growing and James wanted to open another shop on the west side of town. This could be Jay's opportunity to jump careers. James loved the idea of working with Jay and leaving a legacy to his son. Jay took the offer from Dad, and they launched into a partnership.

A variety of income streams gives you more choices in the aging process.

ROOT: Income Streams and Assets
Note: Remember to do proper succession planning with a business.

There was much to consider in a family-owned business. Plenty of people told both James and Jay not to become business partners. They said the business would ruin their relationship as father and son. James and Jay decided to research all the benefits and pitfalls. They even went to a mediator and business consultant to ensure they had clarified roles and responsibilities as well as a strong succession plan. Because James took some of his retirement assets to fund the start of Smith's Speed Shop, he wanted to ensure all the kids were treated equal for inheritance. The operational plan and buy/sell agreement reflected the payment schedule to repay the borrowed funds from James' retirement. The business would be Jay's since he is an actual partner with James. James and Joy went to their estate attorney to think through the division of assets considering the business. They came up with a plan to treat all the kids equal while protecting Jay in the business as well.

At this same time, James and Joy purchased long-term care insurance. Health care in the final stages of life can consume many estates. They worked hard all their lives. They wanted to ensure the kids would get the fruit of their labor. They went on The Decision Tree Plan to update their end-of-life decisions.

James and Jay enjoyed their partnership. The business grew and Jay eventually became President. He found someone who could replace the day-to-day operational responsibilities held by his dad for so long. Once the new person was hired and trained, his dad and mom enjoyed the freedom to travel, taking some major trips abroad while also spending time with the grandkids in Seattle and Portland.

Life was good. At 70, James and Joy still had health and enough energy to enjoy their freedom. They were looking forward to another decade of travel and watching the grandchildren's soccer games. James and Joy were unaware of how fast life would change for them.

While his impulsive and fun nature served Richard well in sales, it did not serve him well in planning for the future. Even though Richard and Mary made good money, they did not have much to show for it. Their retirement savings totaled about $200,000. They still owed $100,000 on the house and another $50,000 in auto and credit card debt.

Richard was now 68 and wanted to retire. He realized there was not enough resources for him and Mary to quit. So, he "sold on." He found it more difficult to sell at 68 than when he was younger. He was forced to retire as a sales manager at age 65, but his company allowed him to stay on in sales with straight commissions. With no cushion, Richard could not quit working.

Richard and Mary always thought about getting things in order for the kids in case of death. They just procrastinated. There was no will, no power of attorney, no directives for end of life, and no instructions for the kids about funerals or burial, nothing. Richard was always going to get around to it. Between the time and expense, he kept putting it off. This sometimes bothered Richard. Every now and then he would say, "I will just let Mary and the kids clean up the mess!" That did not comfort Mary much. He thought about leaving his son, Rex, in charge, but there was always a little "disconnect" between the two of them. Richard loved soccer and other sports. Rex was a nerd, not a jock. Rex grew up with the computer age. He was fascinated by the rapidly changing industry and advancements. Richard and Rex didn't necessarily fight, but there was just no real connection.

Brenda, Rex's wife, didn't help the relationship either. She was always cold and distant. Brenda did not make it easy to see the grandchildren. Faith and Joey were budding soccer stars. Richard and Mary could at least go to the games. However, Brenda rarely informed them about when those games were. Richard was a little worried about how Becky and Brenda might get along after his death. Such things bothered him, so he would turn on the television, watch sports, and try not to think about the realities of his life.

Richard also thought his daughter, Becky, would be great to act as their personal representative. With her accounting background, she could sort out his mess. Every now and then, Richard and Mary would talk about a will and end-of-life decisions. Mary nagged him about it. They were not young kids anymore. Richard felt overwhelmed just thinking about how to figure things out. He felt bad for not providing better for Mary in the future. They had a great life. He spent money as fast as it came in. They made some great memories! Now and then he regretted not saving some money for retirement. He was tired. He wanted to be done! He knew the importance of a will and documents for end-of- life decisions. His friends were dying. Every once in a while, a friend died without getting things in order. It was a mess. But he trusted his daughter, Becky to handle things. He did not realize what a mess he was leaving for Becky.

Living Will or Advanced Medical Directive: A legal instrument to give instructions to the medical community regarding life-sustaining decisions.

Rex and Becky, every now and then, would talk about Richard and Mary's plan for end of life. They knew there was no plan. This bothered them. Becky saw firsthand in her accounting firm the mess of no planning. They decided to approach their parents to talk about a will and end-of-life documents. Someone told them this was the 70/40 talk. In other words, that important talk when the parents reach 70 and the kids reach 40 to discuss EVERYTHING moving forward in the aging process. The first part of the meeting went fine. Richard and Mary knew a will would be helpful and needed, especially Mary. When Rex and Becky pressed Richard to make an appointment with an attorney, he just procrastinated. He said he would get around to it, in his timing, on his terms. Rex and Becky gave up nagging him. They were resigned to pick up the pieces. Little did they know the enormous legal and financial issues they would face or the changes that were coming to their family.

Chapter Five
FALL LEAVES

**The Leaves of Life keep falling one by one.
- Edward Fitzgerald**

It was still early when Jay's cell phone went off. The screen told him it was his mom's cell. In the first few words, he could hear the concern in her voice. He had to finish up and get to the hospital. All he knew at this point was that his dad had some sort of "incident." He didn't know how bad it was, but what he did know was that Joy needed him there, now.

Everything happened so fast that Joy was not sure how she made it to the hospital. All she remembered was her friends from the water aerobics class taking control, helping her call Jay, ushering her into the shower, and then driving her to the hospital. Once she got there, she was still in shock and not processing all that was happening around her.

Upon arriving at the hospital, Joy went straight to the emergency room, but because they were checking James in, she was not allowed to join him. It was terrifying, not knowing if he was going to make it or not. She felt so helpless watching people walk into the hospital and everyone going about their business so calmly. Was today the day she became a widow?

Jay and his wife, Sarah, had never had any emergencies with the children, so the whole hospital setting was a lot to take in. Time dragged on and there was no information from the desk, try as they might to get an answer. Joy was distraught and Jay didn't know how to comfort her besides being a firm shoulder to lean on, but that firm shoulder was hard to hold up. He and his dad had a good relationship. They had their ups and downs, yet loved each other deeply. That is what flooded Jay's thoughts now. How bad was this? Had Jay said the things he needed to say? Was he going to have a chance? His thoughts went to Jared. His brother had the most tenuous relationship with their dad. Would he get a chance to say what he needed to say? Jay started to realize he was already thinking of his family as his responsibility. Jay used the time in the waiting room to contact his sister, Jillian, in Seattle and his brother, Jared, in Boise. He had already called his wife, Sarah, on the way over and she was waiting to contact their children until they heard how grandpa was doing.

Joy was finally allowed to see James. What a relief to see him alive and breathing! It took a while for Joy to comprehend all that had just happened and how it would change their lives. As long as she had her husband, she could face anything, or so she thought.

After what seemed like an eternity, the doctor finally clarified what Jay and his mom had been thinking. A stroke. It had not been too severe, but treatment had fallen outside of the time frame needed for

TPA (Tissue Plasminogen Activator) to work its magic. As they would soon find out, James was confused; his speech had clearly been affected. Words were out of order, random or made no sense. The doctor was said this would most likely clear up over the next 12-24 hours. As the doctor continued to share what had happened, Jay focused on what would be the hardest blow to his energetic dad—paralysis on his right side. The doctor wasn't sure if this was going to improve.

Jay stopped hearing anything at this point. If this was the case, it changed things. Although always fit, Joy was a petite woman and his dad was a foot and a half taller, outweighing her by a good 80 to a 100 pounds. She would not be able to care for him in his present state. Jay was quickly realizing that life as they had known it was very different in the blink of an eye.

The doctor went on to say that there was a real possibility of James having multiple strokes or other issues given his present weakness. Try as he might to ask the questions carefully, it was still jarring to hear the doctor ask about any decisions his father may have made when faced with such a situation. Jay realized what the doctor was asking about...what were Dad's wishes?

Jay asked if there was internet access. He could pull up James' Advanced Directive from the cloud files. He let the doctor know that he had the power of attorney and HIPAA documents as well if they were needed. Thank God, his dad had prepared him long ago. Jay knew he had power of attorney to make decisions and he wanted to honor the decisions that Dad had made. He didn't know what he'd do if that were left up to him. Dad had such a zest for life. He would hate lying in a bed for the rest of his days. Jay didn't quite know what to think. He so wanted things to return as before. Jay was looking at this now like a project at work. What were the possible outcomes? What would need to be put in place, and timelines?

End-of-life decision documents are critical in emergency situations to instruct the family and medical community regarding care.

ROOT: End of Life Plan

The information came in fast and furious now. They looked at his paperwork, they asked about insurance benefits for rehab, where his dad would want to recover, and if they would need some home-care services. He couldn't imagine if he would have been hours away like his siblings. Mom would have been lost. Jay sat down next to his mom and threw his arm around her. "Don't worry, we've got this."

A friend finally came and sat with his mom, freeing Jay up to take a step away. He began the process of calling his siblings, updating them, and setting up an opportunity for them to talk together about where things stood, and for his mom to share the Decision Tree Plan that she and James had put together for this eventuality. Jay knew that his sister and brother would appreciate knowing they were following their parent's wishes as they moved forward. His wife, Sarah, finally showed up too, and Jay finally took a breath. He felt as though he had been holding his breath for hours.

James was always the strong one. He couldn't make decisions right now. Joy was thankful that James had the foresight to discuss various health scenarios with her and what his wishes were in case of just such an emergency. It helped give her peace of mind that she knew what he would want, and that they had filed all the paperwork, so Jay had access to it through the cloud. She may not understand how it all worked, but was thankful for the easy access to the information.

Even though Joy had peace about the decisions regarding James' care, she was concerned about how much James could understand. He woke up from a long nap. He was confused and his conversation did not make any sense. The doctors assured her this was normal. They would just have to wait for any signs of improvement. Joy was worried about James and wondering what kind of life he was going to have moving forward. It was so surreal. She kept thinking, "Can this really be happening? How could her healthy husband end up confused, disoriented, and partially paralyzed?"

That night, as she faced walking out of the hospital and home to her empty house alone, she was scared. While it was comforting to know that Jay and Sarah were close by, they had their own lives to live and three teenagers to raise. Life was busy at their house, and she didn't want to be a burden to them. Joy went home and cried herself to sleep. When she awoke, she was disoriented and wondered where James was. Then she remembered the nightmare yesterday had been and her new reality. There was nothing keeping her home. After a quick shower and breakfast, she went straight to the hospital.

Jay had contacted all the family members. Jillian was coming down from Seattle this morning to meet her at the hospital. It would be comforting to have Jillian by her side.

Jillian had been totally caught off guard yesterday when she heard the news about her dad. Due to the seriousness of his condition, she had decided to take some time off work and stay with Joy. Her children could take care of themselves with her husband's help for a few days. Since James' condition had been stabilized last night, she and her husband decided it was best to wait for the rest of the family to come down.

On the long drive to Portland, Jillian had time to think. Her mind tended to wander to worst-case scenarios, and she thought about all that Dad had done for her through life. She was so thankful that she would be able to see him again. While she had no regrets about their relationship, she wasn't certain she had ever let him know how much she appreciated all that he and Mom had done for the family.

Jillian knew her home situation growing up was not the norm. While she went home every night to a loving family, not all children had that luxury. She and Robert had been modeling that same relationship for their children as well. Once she was down in Portland, she wanted to make sure to let her parents know how much she appreciated the examples they were in her life.

When she finally made it to the hospital, Jillian found her parents together in Dad's room. She started crying, seeing her dad hooked up to so many machines. Jay told her dad had a stroke and was stable. She wasn't prepared for her strong, all-powerful father reduced to needing 24-hour care. He was not even able to sit up in bed. They were limited to see dad while in the ICU. They had to spend most of the day in the waiting room, being admitted every hour or so to check in on him.

After the initial shock of seeing her father, the visits got easier. She and Mom would sit in the waiting area and see him as allowed. Family and friends would drop by, and while visits were limited to immediate family, it was nice to have the distractions of visitors coming to encourage them. She knew Joy appreciated the support of others. Jillian was glad she could go home every night with her mom. The house was lonely and quiet. With Dad stabilizing, Jillian needed to return to Seattle. Her family needed her, too.

The next few days were a little less of a blur as things finally sank in for Jay. The next steps started to take on some clarity. Dad's speech and clear thinking came back, though he certainly had been in a fog. He was moved to a regular room. Then, the hospital wanted to discharge James. How quickly the hospital wanted to discharge his dad surprised and even upset him. Thankfully, dad and mom had considered this possibility in the Decision Tree Plan. They had even picked out a couple of choices. Unfortunately, when Jay called the skilled-nursing communities, there were no openings. The hospital's social worker helped them to secure one. The nurses helped with setting up a transfer to a facility close to his mom and dad's community. This would give dad some time to work on the rehab plan the doctors gave him.

    Jay knew that walking was his dad's main goal. But it was clear to Jay, that once this transfer happened, the clock really began to tick. They had a set amount of time to get dad settled somewhere more permanent. The rehab place could only keep him for 100 days if they stayed within the Medicare guidelines. Dad had made it very clear in their paperwork that mom would not be his caregiver. The idea was comical because of her small size. Mom was committed to Dad, and that meant caring for him if needed. Jay did not doubt that for a second. So, the next steps were laid out for the long term. In the Decision Tree Plan, dad and mom had picked out three care communities. The first two Jay called had no openings, but fortunately, the third had an opening. Jay and mom went over immediately to put down a deposit holding the one-bedroom apartment. Joy checked out the independent living apartments, too. She and James had looked at all the options when doing their initial planning. Now, things were more than planning. They were real.

    Over the coming weeks and months, Jay, Jillian, and Jared were supporting players to their mom as she followed up on the plans she had made with dad. The days included plenty of doctor's appointments and treatments. Dad was a hard worker, which came as no surprise. Dad attacked his physical therapy and speech to regain much of what he lost. They were once again impressed by his tenacity. They were seeing firsthand how the Decision Tree Plan was so helpful during such a stressful time. When the three siblings would get together, they appreciated spending time with dad and mom and not worrying about the details of care.

After James had settled into the rehab facility and his progress began to slow, Joy started worrying about all the details of her life. It was becoming evident that he would not be coming home anytime soon. She was not sure what she would do without the support of her family and friends.

Skilled Nursing: Medical or rehabiliation services provided on a continuous, daily basis in a skilled nursing community.

ROOT: Where Will You Recive Care?

Joy spent most of her waking hours by James' side. She went home every night and wandered around in their large colonial home. She felt lost and alone for the first time in her life. In happier times, Jay, Jillian, and Jared had filled the home with lots of energy and laughter and the house had felt like a home. Even after all the children had left to start their own families, the kids loved to return with their families to fill the house up once again. But now, Joy seriously considered the reality of downsizing. She thought about the independent living apartment she viewed earlier.

As the weeks went by, James began the slow process of learning to talk and walk again. The time had finally come where he was strong enough to transition out of the skilled nursing facility. During the long healing process, Joy had come to realize that their home was not the right fit for them any longer, and she longed for a place to be beside James during the rest of their days together. She was thankful for the planning with James to tour the various continuum-of-care campuses. These care communities included assisted living with resources for memory care and end-of-life, and independent living spaces. Joy was so excited with the idea of living in the same community with James. She would no longer have the daily drive, and still have her own space. She could relax away from the extended care James still needed.

Once the decision was made, Joy realized there was much to be done. She was excited by the opportunity to take on a task again. The kids were glad to see her focus on something other than their dad. They had seen her throw amazing family events, office parties, and fundraisers in the past. They sat back and awaited the ride.

Chapter Six
WINTER AND BARREN BRANCHES

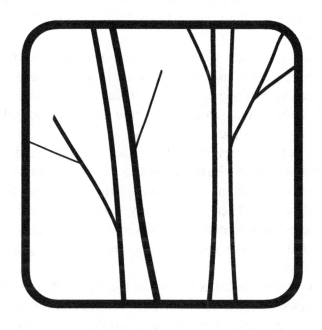

We must be conscious of this: one day, the life we have, will be gone.
- Lailah Gifty Akita

The next morning brought Becky a little more of the reality of her father's death. She had called into work and let them know she would not be able to come in until after the funeral. Becky was overwhelmed with the number of things to do. It was hard to sort out what could wait and what was immediate. She had no idea of her mom and dad's financial situation. She just knew her dad was still doing some work to help.

Richard never thought his financial situation would be discovered. Neither did Mary. Becky had to put that out of her mind right now. There were immediate decisions to make around disposition of the body, funeral arrangements, and final resting place of the remains. Before Mary, Becky, and Rex could go to the appointment at the funeral home, they needed to find out how much money was available. Mary was not very excited about going to the bank with her kids. She knew the bad news.

Richard and Mary were always very private about financial affairs. They were a little embarrassed about it. They should have saved more, prepared more, done more. Now, it was too late. All the decisions that could have been made earlier, were now crisis decisions that MUST be made during grief, shock, and dismay.

Mary was so overwhelmed that making just one decision was enough of a challenge. At the bank, the kids discovered there was $5,000 in checking and $10,000 in savings. Mary felt ashamed for their lack of planning and saving. Richard and Mary would sometimes talk about end-of-life decisions, but nothing was ever written down. Mary thought Richard wanted a regular burial: embalmment, casket, grave, funeral, and memorial stone.

Mary, Becky, and Rex arrived at the funeral home for their appointment. Mary outlined her wishes for the funeral director. She was shocked at the price tag—$10,000 for everything! That would take all her savings. She was still ready to move forward when Becky and Rex asked the funeral director for a few private minutes with their mom. Without knowing any other resources available to their mom, they had to talk to her about alternatives. They could cremate the body. That would only be about $1,000. They could have a private burial with just the family. There would be no need for embalmment and a simple urn would suffice. They could still have a memorial service and invite all their friends and neighbors.

Mary seemed a little combative to Rex and Becky. They had rarely seen that side of their mom. Mary really wanted to have the full funeral service. Mary started raising her voice and became agitated. This was her money, not their money. She could do whatever she wanted. Becky and Rex were embarrassed. They knew others could hear them arguing. Becky and Rex did not know what to do other than support their mom and let her make the decisions. Rex went to get the funeral director, who had stepped out while they discussed their choices. Mary went ahead and planned the funeral experience, spending the full $10,000 in her savings account.

Rex and Becky returned home with Mary. Rex stayed for a while but needed to get back to work. He asked for his sister to walk him out to the car. When they got outside, Rex told Becky they needed some answers, and the sooner the better. He was worried about how Mary acted at the funeral home. She seemed out of character. He wondered about resources to move forward, and how she would handle the finances on her own. Becky felt a great deal of weight as a single mom, studying for her CPA exam, and now the potential added care of her mom. She had no idea the challenges that lie ahead.

Becky gave her mom a break and fixed lunch. After lunch, Becky encouraged her to take a nap. Mary did not sleep much the night before, so a nap felt welcomed. Once Mary closed the door to her bedroom, Becky decided to poke around her dad's home office. His office reflected his life—fun and not much organization. There were some old soccer trophies, team pictures, and other sports memorabilia. Becky opened some drawers looking for important papers—stocks, bonds, life insurance, mutual funds, IRAs, anything. She couldn't even find the payments that were due each month. There was so much clutter; it was hard to dig through it all. The more she dug, the more discouraged she became.

Just then, she turned around and there was her mom standing in the doorway. "What are you doing?" she demanded.

"Oh, I was just trying to organize some of dad's things while you were napping," Becky replied. "Do you feel up to helping me?" Becky could tell Mary did not look happy about her being in the office.

"No, and I think you need to get back to your own business," Mary said somewhat sternly.

Becky felt a little hurt. She was just trying to help. Later that evening, Becky stepped outside so she could call her brother. She told him about the lack of discovery and her mom's stern words to her. Rex told her they better just lay low and get through the funeral. The next few days were filled with family, friends, and neighbors stopping by to bring food, flowers, and condolences. Becky was a little concerned again when her mom could not remember certain people who stopped by and even some of the details needed for the obituary. The day of the funeral finally arrived—the longest day in history. There would be a light lunch at the funeral home for the family and a few close friends, then the final viewing, funeral, and graveside service. After trying to figure out the officiate for the funeral, Mary settled on a close friend of Richard's. People filed by to give their last respects by the open casket. Mary could not believe he was gone. Just like that, everything in her world changed forever. What would she do? How could she go on? Richard did everything for her. She worried every now and then, but Richard's fun-loving way always put her at ease.

Finally, everyone had said their final farewells to Richard and the coffin was closed. The service began. Richard's friend did a wonderful job. Everyone said so. He recited a poem at the end of the service and people came by one more time to give hugs and warm embraces. Mary tried to take it all in, but she felt so numb. It was hard to feel anything but the overwhelming grief that was consuming her. Becky and B.J. drove her to the graveside following the hearse. Becky and Rex had both prepared a few words for the graveside. They each broke down a few times laboring to get the words out. Rex concluded the service, and taking the rose off his boutonniere, he laid it on the coffin. Rex's kids went by and laid a rose on the coffin. Then, it was Becky's turn with B.J.. Finally, Rex and Becky both helped their mom take her rose and lay it on the coffin. It was done. Mary began sobbing, almost heaving. Rex and Becky just held her for what seemed like a lifetime. Mary was finally ready to go. They walked silently down to the cars from the graveside and drove back to the house.

Joy, knowing she would be downsizing and wanting her children to share in the memories of their home, invited all her children over for one of her famous barbecues. Miraculously, they found a weekend that all her children, spouses, and grandchildren could come together. The family gathering together always warmed her heart. Joy arranged for a 30-minute dash to put their names on anything not already tagged with her or James' name on it. Everyone laughed out loud hearing Amy as she put her name on the toaster because "Toast is always better at Grandma's house."

Everything was happening so fast, yet it all made sense. Joy was comforted with all the children and grandchildren together. They even got an informal family picture taken. The photo captured a memory of transitioning, though not planned, the right next step. Joy called an organizer, mover, estate people, and a realtor. The professionals worked together to downsize and stage the house for sale. Within a month, the house was sold! She was thankful for the work done on the Decision Tree Plan to make things easier. Now, the family could focus on family and spending time together making memories.

Joy caught herself looking forward to the new community. She could choose to eat at the traditional dining room, or two different restaurants on campus. Joy's one-bedroom apartment had a full kitchen, washer and dryer, a den, and a full bathroom. The apartment was a big step down from her family home, but large enough to spread out in and feel comfortable. The community also had a swimming pool and many other amenities. She could be happy just hanging around the campus.

Joy enjoyed the proximity of being near James with the flexibility of having her own car and independence. She could keep many of her daily activities like getting her hair done from a friend, shopping, and spending time with friends and family. Joy felt such relief to get settled and back into a routine.

Jay and Sarah came over on Sunday evenings. Their sons, Eric and George, were growing up and had their own lives. Amy still came with them occasionally if she didn't have too much homework. Joy usually cooked for them in her apartment, and James came over to join them for dinner. Once a month or so, they visited one of the restaurants on campus. Their new life offered them the flexibility to do different things, without getting James too far away from his comfort zone.

Joy was staying in touch with some of her old friends while making some new ones. One of the new friendships surprised her. Betty, a young single mother, was one of James' caregivers. As a Certified Nursing Assistant, she really cared about her patients and connected well with Joy. She was not much older than her granddaughter, Amy. Betty looked up to Joy for advice and support in navigating her own path through life.

When Joy first moved into the apartment, she hoped for the day James could join her. Joy could see it on the doctor's face; James was not getting any healthier. Though she would never say this out loud, she had her doubts about the future with James. How many years were left? Would she stay in this community, or get a different place to call home?

If she was living alone in good health, she could buy a condo.

Jay and Sarah were very supportive of whatever she wanted. Sarah even offered to go look at condos with her. Her granddaughter, Amy, joked about getting a condo together near Portland State. Then, she would have a place to live next year at college.

Joy's other children thought it best for her to move out of the community. After all, she didn't need the resources, so why should she be paying for them? Because all of them were encouraging Joy to move, she started looking for a condo to purchase. She would look within a short radius of the community to see James daily.

Jay found a realtor to work with Joy. Michelle was young yet experienced. She knew the market well and liked to work with seniors. She was energetic and listened to Joy's needs. Thus, the search began!

Joy had always wanted to live on the water, so she was drawn to the new condos on the waterfront in Portland. One building had floor to ceiling windows that overlooked the river and city. It was a beautiful view, and she thought she could get used to living downtown. The only obvious problem was the distance to James.

After a few weeks of exhausting the market, and looking at everything available, Michelle brought her back to the perfect unit. It was on the tenth floor and the view was amazing. The price went up with each floor. The condo was a one bedroom, but spacious and light and all she really needed. James had always dreamed of waterfront property. Joy was a little sad knowing James would never join her. This seemed like the perfect place for Joy, but something inside her didn't feel right.

That night, as she laid in bed, Joy could not sleep. Buying the condo seemed like such a perfect fit, why was she not at peace with the decision? The more she thought about it, the more she realized why. Being here next to James had been a deliberate choice. She had independence and the care she would need for the rest of her life. She had new friends among the community and staff. She realized the importance of these new friendships, especially Betty. She was building a new support system. Joy could walk to see James with no commute from downtown.

As Joy considered the options, she concluded that while the condo might have been fun under different circumstances, for now, her home was here. She would call Michelle in the morning and let her know. Once she made the decision, rest came easy. She turned over and got a good night's sleep.

While Joy was going through the process for her next steps, James looked back over the preceding months. The decision to give up the family home was not easy. Joy loved providing a beautiful family home for the kids and the grandkids. The change was difficult, but he knew it had been for the best. Her daily trips to visit him wore her out. When she left to drive home in the evening, he saw her fatigue.

James was thankful for their planning, of how they defined thresholds, and why. They knew friends who became caregivers for their spouses. Caregiving without respite wore them out. James was pleased Joy found an apartment within the campus, could easily see him, and allow others to care for him. He was glad to keep his wife, instead of her becoming his caregiver. The condo Joy described on the waterfront sounded like a dream, yet he was glad she chose not to move away from him.

As James got a bit better, he and his son, Jay, talked about investments and various funds. Mainly, this was to ease James' mind. Whenever possible, his other children, Jillian and Jared, were in on these discussions. Jay would never make big decisions without their input. He knew accountability and clarity was important. Besides, he knew the highest hope for all the kids was following the plan of mom and dad. Jay knew mom and mad appreciated their unity. The unity of the kids gave James and Joy peace while creating a legacy.

After deciding not to move into a condo, Joy fully made her little place home. She wore out the carpets to and from James' room. Joy did seem to tire more easily, but she still kept to a busy schedule. She was still driving too, which was a bit of a concern, but she seemed to be doing well with it. James and Joy said if there was an accident, Jay and the rest of them could sit them down for a "frank discussion about the car." The idea of it made Jay laugh, remembering the "frank discussions" about the car when he was a teenager. So far so good. He knew that with so much change, there were pieces of their "old life" that his mom still had to hold onto for now.

Becky gave Mary a few days to just breathe. The funeral was a whirlwind of activity. Now, just like the aftermath of a storm, Mary was left with the clean up. She felt overwhelmed, scared, and very alone, even with Becky and B.J. living with her. She had no idea how much work was left.
Everything was in Richard's name—utilities, credit cards, even the Netflix account. Whatever was not is his name, she needed to change from

joint to her name alone. All that was a hassle, but the foreboding issue was income. How was she going to live? She went to Social Security with Becky to see what benefits she would have from Richard. Because Richard made a good living, she discovered her benefit would be about $2,500 monthly. That would help but would not cover all the expenses.

Becky finally convinced Mary to go through the office. She discovered the mortgage alone was $2,000. They had $10,000 in credit card debt. They did find a small life insurance policy for $50,000. Mary spent all their savings on the funeral. She suddenly felt paralyzed. What was she going to do? Where would she live? How would she live? Who would take care of her? Mary went to her bedroom, closed the door, curled up on the bed, and cradled herself sobbing.

Becky helped Mary slowly slog through all the necessary steps of transition. Names changed on accounts, life insurance submitted, Social Security filed, even speaking with a mortgage lender to accept a late payment while waiting for life insurance and Social Security. Becky sat down with Mary to make a budget. Mary and Richard never lived by a budget. Becky said she could continue living with her and start helping with the groceries. She could pick up a part-time job while studying for her exam.They also factored in that once she was a CPA, her income would be enough to support them, but it could take at least six months to land a job after she passed the exam. The exam was coming up in another month, so they needed to get by until then. They decided to pay off the credit card with the life insurance proceeds. Mary would need to pay the mortgage for a few months before Social Security would kick in. Mary still owed about $200,000 on the mortgage of the house. A Zillow estimate showed the house was worth about $350,000. What she didn't discover until after a late notice came to the house, was a second Home Equity Line of Credit on the home for another $50,000. That was another $300 a month payment. With taxes, insurance, and utilities, she would need about $3,000 monthly for the house. Becky could help with about $2,000 from her part-time job, but that would still leave them about $1,000 short for groceries, car payment, gas, and other expenses.

James lost hope of leaving the assisted living and rejoining Joy. His weakness had not really changed all that much. His main caregiver, Betty, was on day shift and had developed a great relationship with Joy. As for he and Betty, he enjoyed how she could take his verbal jabs and give them right back. This life was different from the active life he and Joy had enjoyed, but the days passed fairly easily.

Unknown to him, James was struggling more than he knew. Some walks and visits with Joy revealed some changes in James. Joy noticed the start of strange comments, confusion, and other signs. Jay realized it, too. On his visits with James, he wanted to review time and again aspects of their planning and would suggest changes to this or that, which were unnecessary.

Jame's gait became rougher and more unsteady. A visit to his neurologist showed the truth. Several small, unrecognized strokes had closed off flow to part of James' brain. The beginning signs of vascular dementia were apparent. The small strokes would likely continue, and the dementia would more rapidly increase.

Jay and Joy moved James into the Memory Care section of the community. Joy still had the freedom to visit. For a short time, Betty would work with James to make that transition easier. The space was smaller, but there was still some room to hang family pictures and art enjoyed by James. The staff shared that familiar items help someone transition more comfortably into new surroundings with less agitation, which can accompany change. The photos and art might help James hold onto his memories.

Jay knew this was the final move for his dad. Every visit was beginning to play out the same as the one before, almost word for word. Dad being such a big guy, Jay was glad that there were no physical outbursts like he had read about in some cases. Jay, his mom, and his siblings, quickly became specialists on dementia. Jay hoped this would not last too long.

Activities of Daily Nursing (ADL): Routine activities that come into play when being assessed for the correct level of care.

ROOT: Where Will You Recive Care? When Will You Recive Care?

Chapter Seven
THE LAST LEAF ON THE TREE

Honor your father and your mother,
that your days may be long in the land that the LORD
your God is giving you.
- Exodus 20:12 ESV

One morning a few short weeks later, James' caregiver Betty went to help him get ready for the day. The usual schedule is breakfast, then his therapy session. She headed up to his room, expecting to hear the news blaring a bit too loudly from behind the door. Instead, she opened the door to silence. The lights were still out in the room. Her heart went up into her throat. James was still in bed. Joy's face was smiling from the picture on the bedside table. Betty went over to the intercom to call down to the office and the day nurse desk. Her mind went to Joy. Who and how would someone break the news? She saw this often, but it never became easier.

Jay was at peace when he got the call from the community that his dad had passed away in his sleep. It was getting harder to see his very strong and able dad lose pieces of himself. The finality of not seeing his dad again was overwhelming and incredibly painful. Yet, at the same time, he was relieved. The family was spared the experience of the latent stages of dementia. Dad left still knowing his family and cherished memories. Once again, Jay found himself making a round of phone calls to help his mom. James was 80. He was a loving husband, father, and grandfather.

Mary and Becky managed for the next six months by spending the life insurance money. Becky continued to notice more problems with Mary's memory. She saw some late notices on the desk. Mary began repeating herself. Then came the day when Becky got a call from the local police. Mary had gone through a red light. When the officer asked her where she was headed, she could not recall. Mary was confused and could not find her way home. Becky had to come and pick her up. Later, Becky and Rex went to get the car. They could no longer ignore the signs of dementia.

Mary was finally convinced to go to the doctor. In the meantime, they took the car keys away. Mary was so upset.

"You had no right to take away my independence."

The tension in the house between Mary and Becky was thick. Mary gave Becky the silent treatment.

The day came for Mary to go to the doctor. It took all of Becky's persuasion skills to convince Mary to follow through with the appointment. Becky had informed the doctor of the car incident, some of Mary's forgetfulness, and other behaviors before the appointment. The doctor gave Mary a cognitive screening test. She was not happy about it but cooperated. Mary scored in the range where her cognitive abilities were impaired. At least now, Becky had some medical evaluation of Mary's health and mental status. Mary was doing fine physically, but mentally? Becky realized she really should be handling the finances. Becky had already tried to offer help in paying bills with Mom. Mary was resistant. She wanted to prove to herself she could do this.

A few months went by. One day Becky came home from running errands and the power was off. She called the power company to report the outage. She discovered the power had been shut off. She walked Mary through the power company situation. Mary could not understand. She was convinced the bills were paid. Becky talked Mary into auto payments on the utilities. The water and gas were in danger of being shut off as well. Becky was worried about the house. Had Mary made her mortgage payments? She watched the mail and saw a letter from the bank. She discovered her mom was in the beginning of foreclosure proceedings.

This time, she could not convince Mary to pay the back mortgage. Becky did not want her mom to lose the house. She called Rex to talk about options. Rex got involved and tried to convince Mary to pay the back mortgage. They showed Mary the foreclosure letter from the bank, but she just thought they forged the document to get money from her. She threatened to kick Becky and B.J. out. Her personality was changing with the dementia. She would never talk this way to her children.

Becky and Rex met to determine next steps. They both realized their mom could no longer handle the finances and they needed to intervene.

Without Mary's cooperation, and no power of attorney papers in place, they had to contact an eldercare attorney. After a consultation with the attorney, they had no choice but to begin conservatorship and guardianship proceedings.

The attorney contacted the bank on their behalf. The bank suspended proceedings until after the court decided on the conservatorship. It was a long month at the house for Becky living with Mary. Mary secured an attorney to fight the conservatorship proceedings. Things were quickly going south. Mary was using the remaining funds from the life insurance to pay attorney bills.

Conservator/Guardian: A court appointed fiduciary where one is responsible for the financial and/or physical well-being of a protected person.

ROOT: Wills and Estate

By the time Becky won conservatorship and guardianship rights to Mary, there was no money left. She and Rex were left with no choice but to put the house up for sale. They soon realized Becky could not take care of her mom as she continued to deteriorate. Becky had passed the CPA exam during all the craziness. She was looking for a job and could not work and take care of Mary.

Mary's dementia was not severe enough for memory care, but she could not live on her own. Her choices were limited. The funds from the home sale could quickly be consumed in a memory care community. Thus far, Mary was not aggressive nor was she wandering. Becky used a placement agency to help locate an adult foster home that might meet their needs for Mary. They found a home that could accommodate Mary at this point, and hopefully, even as she progressed. Rex was not convinced about the adult foster home. Rex wanted Mary in a care community. They had some sharp words over the conflict. Becky was the one who had both conservatorship and guardianship rights. She hated to go against Rex, but it was her legal decision. She chose the adult foster home. Rex refused to help move Mary. In fact, he cut off all communications with Becky.

Becky felt incredibly alone and overwhelmed. The day came to move Mary into the adult foster home. Mary was resistant and mean. The day was horrible. Becky felt horrible. She resented her mom and dad for this whole difficult process. If they would have done some planning, so much of this could have been averted. Now, Becky was faced with getting the home ready to sell, starting a new job, and trying to secure housing for herself and B.J.. On top of that, everything took more time because she was representing Mary. She had to fax the conservatorship papers to all the professionals involved in the sale of the home. But what surprised her was the difficulty with the bank. She jumped through so many hoops just to get money to pay the bills.

Becky started to sort through everything at the house. There was so much stuff! Rex was not speaking to her or helping in any manner.

After a week of working through the papers in the home office, she cried uncle. She asked her attorney for some recommendations for professionals who could help her. She decided on an organizer who could help sort, sell, and dispose. Perfect! The organizer met with her on a Saturday. They decided on a plan of action. The organizer and her team went to work. By the end of the week, the house was cleared except for the furniture needed for staging. She could not believe it! The realtor gave her some tips on what to fix and what to leave. A handyman was called who could complete all the necessary repairs. The house went on the market.

Becky tried to see Mary at least three times weekly. It was hard to see her mom in another setting. The foster home provider was great and worked hard to help Mary adjust. At the beginning, Mary was still mad and barely said anything to Becky, so she decided to bring B.J. with her. That was helpful because Mary would at least respond to him. By the time the house was on the market, Mary was adjusting and conversing with Becky. Fortunately, the house sold within 30 days. The closing would be another 30 days out. Now Becky had to find housing for herself. Becky decided on a nice two-bedroom apartment near B.J.'s school.

The last daunting task was selling everything left in the home and moving her and B.J.'s things to the new apartment. She called the organizer again and prepped for an estate sale. They agreed anything not sold would be donated. Rex still was not speaking with Becky and did not believe the house must be sold. The chasm deepened between them. Not only was she losing her mom to dementia one day at a time, but she was also losing her brother as well. Life sucked! If only her parents had invested in some end-of-life planning.

The estate sale came and went. Becky and B.J. got moved. Becky closed on the house, paid the bank, and placed the remaining funds in the bank under the supervision of the court according to the conservatorship instructions. If Mary's needs did not increase, she would have enough funds for about three years of care. Mary's body was strong, but her mind was weak. She could outlive her resources. Because she would privately pay for at least a couple of years, the foster home would keep her if she went on Medicaid. That was a real comfort to Becky.

James death hit Joy harder than she expected. It seemed to happen so suddenly, even though looking back, it was a blessing that he didn't suffer more than he did. She went through the motions of taking care of all the details, the memorial service, and all the visiting that went with the grieving process. She was thankful James had planned for his service and she knew exactly what he wanted. The decisions were made and easily accessible through the cloud files. As the family returned to their busy lives, and friends were caught up in their own activities, Joy began to lose interest in life. She had no energy, and no desire to go anywhere. Joy spent more time in her apartment, sleeping and missing James.

Jay especially was worried about her and encouraged mom to get out. One day, after his insistence that she leave her apartment, she ventured out to the garden. It was a beautiful day, and a little fresh air would be good for her. She went outside and sat on a bench just looking at the flowers. But her James was gone. They had been so perfect together and he had been everything to her. She found no joy in life any longer.

Getting up from the bench, she started back to her apartment. The path that led through the garden was wide, but Joy wasn't paying attention. She began to wander off the path, and her foot landed sideways on the edge of the pavement. Her foot twisted under her and she crumpled to the ground.

An ambulance was called and Joy was rushed to the same hospital that treated James. The diagnosis came, she had shattered her hip and would need surgery. Physically, Joy was in good shape and they had an opening in the surgery schedule.

Once again, Jay found himself at the hospital, this time, waiting for his mom to come out of surgery. Time seemed to drag, and there was no news from the doctors. After hours of waiting, the doctor appeared. He had a defeated look on his face. The surgery took longer than expected, and in the process Joy's heart had stopped, and they couldn't save her. He was sorry, but they did all they could for her.

Jay was sad, but not surprised. His mom had really been missing his dad. He saw her zeal for life ebb away in grief and loneliness. She was finally reunited with her James.

Jay made all the required phone calls, and the family came together. The service for Joy would be like James'. Mom had planned all the details in advance and left no questions unanswered. It would be a simple affair with family and friends celebrating a life well lived.

The dreaded day came on a bright spring morning when Becky went to visit Mary. Mary did not recognize her. She knew the day was coming. Her mom's dementia was a steady, deadly march erasing her memory and ultimately, her ability to stay alive. Becky still came to visit Mary. She introduced herself and became friends at each visit. Sentences became more difficult.

It was terrible to admit, but Becky was grateful when Mary contracted pneumonia. The continual decline of Alzheimer's was brutal and the eventual death was not kind. Mary became weaker from the pneumonia. The doctor suggested that hospice be called. Becky came every day at this point. Death was not far away.

After only a week or so, the hospice nurse called both Rex and Becky. Mary was struggling. Becky and Rex hugged and held hands at her bedside watching life ebb away. Mary was gone. Becky wanted Rex to help her plan the funeral. It was so good to have her brother back. They decided on cremation and a simple ceremony. Mary loved the beach. They decided to scatter her ashes in the ocean.

On a windy, sunny day off the Oregon coast, Becky, B.J., Rex, and his family rented a small whale watching boat to take them out of the harbor to scatter their mom's ashes. They had purchased a small boat to place her ashes in. Together, the family took turns saying goodbye to Mary. Rex launched the boat in the water. The boat drifted off in the distance carried by the current. They headed back to shore.

As Becky reflected on the past several years, she decided to create all the necessary legal and financial documents for herself and B.J.. She did not want B.J. to walk through all the chaos she experienced with her dad and mom. She realized one of the most loving things she can do for B.J. is planning for her eventual death.

Part Two
The Honor Your Parent Process

Chapter Eight
ROOT ONE: WILLS AND ESTATES

The best way to achieve any goal is to have a written plan. A goal that isn't written down is just a dream.
- Dave Ramsey

According to a 2015 Rocket Lawyer estate-planning survey by Harris Poll, 64% of Americans don't have a will. Of those without a plan, about 27% said there isn't an urgent need for them to make one — and 15% said they don't need one at all. As we saw in the case of Richard and Mary, without a will and accompanying end-of-life documents, the work for the heirs becomes complicated. The extraordinarily wealthy entertainer Michael Jackson died without a will, in other words, intestate. It took years to sort out his estate through a bitter family fight. One of the most loving things you will do for your family or friends is prepare for death. They need to grieve, not sort through the laws and regulations of probate.

WILLS

There are many reasons people do not draw up wills; time, money, and avoiding mortality are a few. For many Americans, a simple will with Durable Power of Attorney and end-of-life instructions can be created by a local attorney for a modest sum. Any type of will is better than no will at all.

At Genesis Mediation, we have helped families sort out several issues from businesses to investments because a will was not in place or too vague. You need to remember that some investments, e.g. life insurance and retirement accounts, are governed by the designation of beneficiaries that will override the instructions in a will to the personal representative. I have one story where a husband died leaving a million-dollar life insurance policy to his ex-wife of more than 20 years because he did not change the beneficiary. His present wife of 15 years was not happy!

The basic elements of a will include:
 - Sufficient information to identify you
 - Appointment of a Personal Representative or Executor
 - Who are your beneficiaries? This can be people and/or charities.
 - How to disburse your assets to the beneficiaries
 - Naming guardians for minor children
 - Two people to witness your signing of the will
 - Cognitive competence
 - Over the age of 18

If one has minor children, leaving the appointment of guardians and funds for care and education are very practical. Many young couples may not have much in the form of assets, yet can provide for each other and the children through life insurance. In the unfortunate and rare event of the death of both parents, the guardians have clear directions for the care of the children. The will can instruct the personal representative to set up a trust for the children and assistance for the guardians.

Let's say a young couple has two children and between both the husband and wife, a million dollars of life insurance. Upon death, the personal representative can set up a trust for the children. Provisions can be made for an immediate advance to the guardians to help secure a larger home, if needed. The guardians could use the interest generated by the funds to help with the care of the children. Then, as the children reach 18, the trust can help with educational efforts.

Without a trust, the entire amount of the insurance policy is given to the beneficiary at age 18. Giving an 18-year-old half a million dollars may not be a wise decision! Often, a parent may select three different ages for a distribution from the trust such as age 22, 28, and 32. The adult child has three opportunities to use the funds wisely. Thus, if each child received $500,000, let's say $100,000 is used for education. That leaves $400,000. The child then receives a third of the remainder at age 22, or $133,000. That is still quite a sum for a 22-year-old. The child may wish to pursue more education, which the funds could be applied or used to help purchase a home. At age 28, the child will receive another $133,000. Then, at 32, a final distribution. If the child makes some mistakes with money earlier, there is one last opportunity to invest the funds more wisely.

TRUSTS

Trusts are varied and created to assist the trustmaker and heirs to avoid probate and preserve wealth. We highly recommend you make an appointment with an estate attorney to discuss which trust is best for your situation. Trusts are either revocable or irrevocable and used for either asset protection or to minimize tax, or both. The following is a brief overview of some trusts.

A Living Trust or Revocable Trust

Revocable Trusts, often called a Living Trust, are created during the lifetime of the trustmaker. The trust can be altered, changed, modified, or revoked entirely. Revocable trusts are extremely helpful in avoiding probate. Many revocable trusts evolve into an irrevocable trust upon the death of the trustmaker.

Irrevocable Trust
The purpose of this trust is wealth preservation from estate and gift tax. The estate is often split between two parties, usually husband and wife. When one party passes, say the husband, who has the "A" trust, the trust evolves into an irrevocable trust. The wife is the trustee, with a child often in second position. The other party, the wife with trust "B" can use the funds from trust "A" for health and basic living costs. When the wife passes, the "B" trust becomes irrevocable. An estate attorney can assist you in creating and explaining this type of trust.

Special Needs Trust
A special needs trust is useful for those within the Medicaid system to ensure they remain eligible. For example, my brother is disabled. My father set up a provision within his will for me, the personal representative, to establish a special needs trust. My brother cannot allow more than a modest amount in his bank account or assets or he will be disqualified for benefits. There are numerous regulations surrounding how to use funds from a special needs trust. Mainly, one cannot use funds for either rent or food.

Income Cap Trust
An income cap trust is established to assist the trustmaker to retain limited assets and income while transitioning to Medicaid. The trust allows Medicaid right of recovery in first position as claimant. The trustmaker can set up the trust for his or her own benefit.

Charitable Trust
Charitable Trusts are trusts which benefit a particular charity or the public in general. Most people establish a charitable trust as part of an estate plan to lower or avoid estate and gift tax. A charitable remainder trust (CRT) funded during the grantor's lifetime can be a financial planning tool, providing the trustmaker with valuable lifetime benefits. Those who establish a CRT enjoy philanthropic efforts and the concept of a gift that continues to give after death. You can also create a charitable lead trust (CLT) which provides benefits to a charity for a period of time before the balance is available to the remaining beneficiaries, usually children or grandchildren.

Spendthrift Trust
A spendthrift trust is often created by a parent for a child who struggles to manage assets. The beneficiary cannot sell or pledge interests of the trust. The trust is protected from creditors. The beneficiary can enjoy the funds generated by the trust but cannot touch the trust itself. The trust is distributed upon the death of the named beneficiary. This is often a clause within a trust.

Skip Generation Trust
Grandparents who wish to gift assets to their grandchildren can use a skip generation trust. The parents are usually the trustees of the trust. They may or may not use proceeds generated by the trust. Depending upon the instructions of the trust, the grandchildren may receive disbursements from the trust at certain ages or at the death of the trustee(s).

DROP DEAD FILE

We see many scenarios at Genesis Mediation and Honor Your Parent. A very common one is the husband has made plans to care for his wife after death. However, he has never adequately communicated to her the details of finances and final wishes. She is not aware of the entire estate, where to find papers of financial records and accounts, life insurance policies, and the list goes on. She needs to grieve, but instead she spends endless hours tracking down everything and wondering, did she miss something? She never built a relationship with their financial advisor. Her husband always took care of that. Now she needs to rely upon very important financial advice from a stranger. If the husband had created a Drop Dead File for his wife, it could make all the difference. Here are a few recommendations to help a spouse after your passing:

- Set up and constantly update your Drop Dead File. Make sure your end-of-life decisions and wishes are included as well as your digital footprint and passwords to accounts.
- Cover any changes with your spouse.
- Review the file at least quarterly.
- Build a relationship with your professionals which includes your spouse, especially the attorney and financial advisor.

Your spouse needs a child or trusted friend to help him or her. This person should know everything in your Drop Dead File and Honor

Your Parent Plan to come along side your spouse. Upon death, when your spouse is grieving, it is difficult to make decisions clearly. Only necessary decisions should be made immediately. Defer as many as possible.

GUARDIANSHIPS AND CONSERVATORSHIPS

The appointment of who will have Power of Attorney is an extremely important decision. You need to trust this person explicitly. He or she will handle all your financial and health matters, if given the Health Power of Attorney and Advanced Medical Directive as well. When someone is not appointed with legal authority for financial or health decisions, things become complicated quickly. Without proper legal direction, your loved ones will need to begin guardianship and conservatorship proceedings with an attorney. This is very expensive, time consuming, and can cause conflict within the family. Sometimes there are not appropriate choices within the family for guardianship or conservatorship, thus the court will appoint a professional fiduciary.

In a conservatorship, a concerned friend or family member may see the need for someone to protect an individual who may no longer be able to make wise decisions regarding his or her finances and physical well-being. When there is no family or friends, the state social services agency may step in and push for protection. This may be a result of concerned entities such as banks, title companies, or doctors. The bottom line is when proper planning has not taken place, the process of putting someone in place becomes a question for the court.

In the appendix, you will find a variety of tools that can help you check to see if a loved one or friend may have concerns regarding capacity. Capacity is the cognitive ability to make wise decisions for oneself. Ultimately, a review by a neurologist and interviews with concerned individuals in the person's life will play a role in deciding whether protection is ordered by the court.

There are professional fiduciaries who can also fill a variety of roles in helping individuals manage and protect assets as well as step in to make medical decisions when others are not available. Different states may have different names for each role, but an individual put in place to make decisions regarding the physical well-being and care is the guardian. A conservator is one who has legal authority to manage the financial affairs of an individual's assets/estate.

To start the process, there is a petition made to protect an individual. The individual or respondent can challenge the petition. A "court visitor," a trained professional, will make the interviews necessary to give expert testimony before the court. A judge ultimately decides the need for a conservator, guardian, or both. Family is often the first choice in the appointment of a guardian or conservator for the "protected person." A protected person is a designation of the court. If a family member is unwilling or unable to serve as the guardian or conservator, the court will appoint an individual chosen by the family from referrals provided by the elder law attorneys serving the case.

    The conservator/guardianship process stays in place until the individual passes away and the executor or trustee takes over. They will make all decisions that support the physical and financial well-being of the protected person. The duties of a professional fiduciary include learning the desires and wishes of the protected person. Thus, he or she can make decisions aligned with the wishes of the protected person if he or she had capacity. All fees for attorneys, court, and professional fiduciaries appointed are paid from the assets of the protected person. The process and costs of the appointment of guardians and conservators is expensive, time-consuming, and potentially conflict-laden. One of the most loving things you will do for your loved ones is preparing for aging and death to avoid this process. When you plan, your wishes are followed by those you direct.

Chapter Nine

ROOT TWO: INCOME STREAMS AND ASSETS

Never depend upon a single income. Make investment to create a second source.
- Warren Buffet

The ability to create and maintain income during the retirement years is critical to expanding your choices around quality and type of care. If there are few resources, your choices will narrow to Medicaid allowances. If you can provide private pay for communities and resources, there will be many available options. The average baby boomer is trying to retire on $25,000 in savings.

One thing to think about is that we are living longer. In the United States, life expectancy for men is now 76.4 years, and for women it is 81.2. This combination of longer life expectancy with fewer resources will place a great deal of pressure on our social systems. The silver tsunami is quickly approaching, with more than 10,000 baby boomers retiring every day. How can you survive and thrive in retirement?

In our story, Mary enjoyed a good life with Richard during the earning years. However, because they were not saving and preparing for retirement, when Richard died she was left in crisis. The active income stream was no longer available and passive income was not sufficient to sustain the lifestyle or even a shadow of their previous life. Mary could sell her house and live for a time on the equity. Others, who have no real estate or other investments, can become homeless within months, or even weeks. In our work at Genesis Mediation and Honor Your Parent, we often see the spouse, usually the wife, fall into poverty and limited to the benefits of Medicaid, which are very minimal and restrictive. If a child or family member does not help with housing and aid, life becomes very difficult. With the coming silver tsunami, the strain on Social Security, Medicare, and Medicaid will reach crisis proportions.

Creative solutions are on the horizon for alternatives. However, we do not recommend your solution to be government aid. Even if you are approaching retirement, there are some strategies to help keep you out of poverty.

ACTIVE INCOME STREAMS

The first choice many make is working into retirement age, which is shifting. For Social Security purposes, you can begin to collect benefits at age 62, which in the future may be reduced as much as 30%. If you wait until the retirement age designated by social security, you will receive your full benefit.

If you wait until age 70, you can increase your benefit by earning delayed retirement credits. However, most people choose to work because they do not have sufficient savings or resources to support themselves. Unfortunately, many people end up working as long as possible to make ends meet, then fall into Medicaid for assistance when they can no longer work.

When meeting with a financial planner to consider retirement options, you will be surprised how long you can retain and extend resources when coupled with active income. Many Baby Boomers think about retirement more as a shift of work intensity and variety rather than total retirement. There is an entire movement of sprouting entrepreneurs of those over 55 as boomers seek choices to control their own time and work rhythm. Some enjoy the ability to freelance in their own respective field of expertise, while others go for the full startup of a business. Many boomers find it attractive to leverage their experience and age as a positive in business rather than a liability in the workplace. Ask those searching for a job at age 60 about the available offerings, other than low paying retail options.

For example, Joe was let go by major technology company at age 60 in a downsizing. Between company stock options and the 401(k) investments, Joe could retire. However, as he sat down with his financial planner, it could be tight depending upon life choices and expectancy. He selected to use some of his resources to start up an independent computer repair, networking, and consultation service geared for small businesses. His years of experience and problem solving was very valuable to his clients. And because he was not trying to build a large business, just pay the bills, he could offer very competitive rates. When he reached out for assistance in the formation and marketing of the business, he relied on other Boomers, some of whom were starting their own consulting businesses. Joe had a full year of severance from the company. Within that year, he began to build his new business. He joined a few networking groups, learned to use social media, and launched a website. By the end of year two, Joe was paying his basic bills along with the part-time job of his wife. One year later, he replaced most of his income with the flexibility of a business owner.

Joe quickly realized the need for an associate to help when he and Joanne wanted to travel. He wanted someone to succeed him in the business as well. The idea of legacy was attractive to Joe. He found someone much younger who wanted to eventually take over the company. They worked out a plan of succession that represented the interests of both by using a mediator. By this simple plan, Joe extended his resources by a decade. He worked in his business until age 70. His resources continued to grow as well as the business. Joe self-funded the buyout of the business and avoided a large tax bill on the sale while creating another income stream in full retirement. Joe even consulted every now and then for his protégé. He enjoyed mentoring and the new owner appreciated his wisdom!

Some form of active income can greatly assist most people to extend their resources longer into retirement while giving them funds for travel or other desired life choices. Money is not everything, but enough of it certainly helps expand decisions in the aging process.

REAL ESTATE

Real estate can be very effective in creating passive income for retirement. Even a few rentals can be helpful in contributing to cash flow and overall assets. The best time to purchase rentals is earlier in life. Let the renters pay the mortgage, with the goal of no debt at retirement. Typically, during the earning years one does not need the cash flow. Upon retirement, the owner now has an asset with no liability, plus cash flow. Whether condos, houses, duplexes or small multi-family units, real estate can be a valuable part of a portfolio and income stream.

A popular movement in real estate is Additional Dwelling Units (ADU's). Some cities are making exceptions for codes and taxes. An ADU is a small dwelling that can be an addition to a current structure, a temporary unit, or a permanent unit. The usual strategy is the owner of the larger home moves into the small unit in retirement and rents out the home. Some ADUs are converted containers that can be very attractive and functional. The cost of the ADU compared to purchasing a separate property is sizable. The party already owns the land, and the ADU typically can tie into existing utilities. If you enjoy travel and will not spend a great deal of time in the dwelling, this is a simple way to help fund the travel and extend resources into retirement.

An important decision in the aging process is selling or retaining the residential home of your parents if they move into a community. The comparison spreadsheet in the appendix would be helpful to determine the results of either action. If sufficient revenue can be generated between rent of the residence along with other resources to fund care, some may choose to rent and preserve the real estate asset. One can either manage the property or use a property management company. People do not often realize the property management company will take on many of the headaches of a landlord for a modest price. If the needed monthly cash flow outstrips rent and other resources, normally the house must go up for sale.

With the silver tsunami of Boomers hitting retirement age, there will be more choosing to age in place with other Boomers. Boomers can rent out rooms of their large homes after raising kids, then share in hiring caregiving as needed. This will become an attractive option for those with limited funds who wish to remain as independent as possible in a home venue. With shared housing and caregiving, some situations will provide room, board, and salary for a caregiver.

PENSIONS

When pensions were popular, the average lifespan of a male, who was the primary provider, was 67 years old. Companies realized they would end up with a positive amount in the pension fund. As pensions continued and longevity increased, pension funds could not sustain members living 20 years past retirement. Before the Great Recession, General Motors had more people drawing pension than actively working. Most companies or public plans now have a mix between pension and a 401(k), or no pension offered at all.

If you are fortunate enough to have a pension, the monthly payment can be very helpful as an income stream to fund care. Most pensions can cover partial, if not all, the cost of basic care in a community. With a few other added pieces to the income stream, choices for care are increased for those who can privately pay.

SOCIAL SECURTIY

Social Security was instituted in 1935[1]. The original intent of Social Security was to provide retired workers over the age of 65 an on-going income[2]. Social Security is a moving target, subject to the passage of new laws by Congress. Here is a brief overview. For more detailed information, contact your local Social Security center or search www.ssa.gov.

You can begin receiving your Social Security benefit as early as 62 years of age, or as late as 70. If you claim it early, at 62, your benefit will be reduced. If you claim it late, at 70, your benefit will be maximized. You can calculate your retirement age, when you will receive

---

1 Social Security "Social Security History," Social Security, accessed February 16, 2017, https://www.ssa.gov/history/orghist.html.
2 "Social Security History"

100% of your benefit, according to the Social Security Administration by visiting www.socialsecurity.gov/planners/retire/ageincrease.html.

Survivors benefits can be complicated with the Social Security Administration. If your spouse dies, you will typically receive some or all of the benefit, depending upon how much you are currently receiving from Social Security. A surviving spouse can begin receiving benefits as early as age 60, or age 50 if disabled. If the deceased spouse elected to draw benefits early, at age 62, then the surviving spouse cannot receive the full amount based on retirement age.

It is important to apply for benefits quickly. The Social Security Administration may choose to begin payments at application instead of death. You will need a death certificate, social security number of both the deceased and yourself, your birth certificate, and marriage certificate. If you are divorced but were married for more than 10 years, you may be able to claim benefits from your ex-spouse. Contact the Social Security Administration for more details.

Social Security will rarely meet the monthly living expenses without supplemental income. Far too many Americans are falling into Medicaid, medical care provided by the government for those with modest means. Medicare is the government health insurance system for those who have sufficiently paid into the Social Security system. Medicare is very helpful to curb extreme health costs to those over 65. Combined with a supplemental health insurance provider, health costs can be modest. The exceptions can be expensive pharmaceuticals not covered by Medicare or the supplemental insurance provider. You will find additional information in the appendix related to supplemental insurance for Medicare. The choices can be confusing.

Social Security Income is provided for those who meet the qualifications of Social Security for disability. SSI is provided for those with modest means who have not sufficiently invested into the Social Security system. This income can ONLY be used for food and shelter. The stipend is rarely sufficient to cover actual costs of food and rent. The recipient is restricted to any funds or assets not greater than $1500. Parents with children classified as disabled by Social Security typically set up some form of Special Needs Trust or other trust to provide for their child's needs that will be accepted by Social Security. Special Need Trusts are touched upon in the Wills and Estates Root system.

Social Security Disability Income is provided for those who meet the criteria of disability by Social Security AND have sufficiently paid into the Social Security system. The income received by the recipient is often greater than SSI and carries no restrictions for use or asset retention. In other words, you can have far above $1500 in assets and receive SSDI.

Social Security can certainly aid in retirement and aging. However, one simply cannot rely upon Social Security to provide for all needs in your later years. The payments of Social Security and medical assistance can play into the overall retirement and aging plan. One must understand how some provisions may shift by new laws or policies.

INVESTMENTS

Investments are many and varied. Scheduling an appointment with a Certified Financial Planner with expertise and a breadth of knowledge is highly recommended.

In order to fund the growing financial needs in the aging process, investments earlier in life are necessary. Many companies offer 401(k) or non-profits a 403(b) plan. Individually, there are various types of IRAs for investment. One can select the risk and type of investments within these retirement vehicles. At the time of this writing, depending on lifestyle choices, most investment planners state the average couple needs between $1,000,000 and $2,000,000 along with no debt plus long-term care insurance to carry them from retirement to end of life.

Financial planners will vary in investment strategy. They will interview you, consider your goals and lifestyle choices, and then recommend some selections within an overall plan. Some planners like certain stocks or bonds, some will recommend annuities, others will even suggest a little diversity in precious metals or other similar investment.

Some people are fortunate in gaining an inheritance or a lump sum settlement. This sudden influx of wealth can be difficult to navigate. One can read the horror stories of many lottery winners. Parents can worry about a child quickly spending the funds and ending up destitute. Parents should consider options by a financial planner and estate attorney to determine the best course of action for inherited monies.

Tax consequences on investments is also important to consider, pre-retirement or post-retirement. An appointment with a CPA or CFP is helpful to determine tax implications for all investments, including real estate.

CASH FLOW AND BUDGETS

All the assets and income streams mentioned above create cash flow. The Decision Tree Plan can instantly let your loved ones know what is needed for monthly cash flow, recurring bills, and your budget. The cash flow and budget spreadsheet allow visibility to ensure income sources continue to flow and bills are paid. When I needed to step in to assist my mom with finances, understanding income sources as well as bills was very important to maintain her lifestyle. Once I needed to move her to an adult foster home, I knew how much she would require from her savings to pay the difference between income and cost of care. She immediately entered a spend down cash position. She had sufficient resources for two years of private pay before moving to Medicaid. Notifying siblings of the spend down helps them understand there will most likely be no inheritance. Communication and transparency is always a good rule in dealing with the finances of a parent or loved one with other siblings. This can help avoid conflict over finances.

Chapter Ten

ROOT THREE: END OF LIFE DECISIONS

Life is what happens to us while we are making other plans. - Allen Saunders

While there are challenges along the road to planning your aging process, inevitably that road leads to a very emotional end-of-life decisions. End-of-life decisions can seem morbid and depressing. When we ask people why they keep putting off these decisions, they simply say, "I don't want to deal with it." We have found just the opposite to be true. When people plan these critical decisions, and inform others, they feel empowered. The family is also grateful when the time comes to carry out the decisions. They are following the directions of a loved one, not guessing what to do. And, when we let others know our wishes, it is one of the most loving final acts we convey. Children can honor their parents.

End-of-life decisions include control over our physical and legal being, what we want to happen when we die, and who and how to take the steps necessary when the time comes. In this section, you will find areas that you might have considered, and possibly some you have not. For example, in our technological age, we now need to consider things like passwords, social media accounts, and our overall digital footprint.

ONLINE AND DIGITAL PROPERTY CONCERNS

An online poll by Intel Security showed that the average adult now has 27 online accounts to manage. That means 27 usernames and passwords[1] to keep organized. We all know how frustrating it can be when we get locked out of one of our accounts. However, even if one is locked out, business marches on. In the face of crisis or loss, how quickly can we get into necessary accounts?

Estate attorneys are concerned about access to digital property. In the Decision Tree Plan, allowing full access to your digital property may help lower administration costs or fees. Furthermore, it will ensure that no valuable or significant digital property is overlooked in the moment of crisis.

Unlike traditional types of property, digital property and social networks may have additional, significant obstacles for executors, fiduciaries, and family members if passwords are unavailable. These obstacles range from the obvious usernames and passwords to existing laws regarding computer access and privacy. They can make it practically impossible to access your digital property.

---

1 Survey Says People Have Too Many Passwords. Bruce Snell, Buzzfeed Tech, May 2016

How should you plan? Make a list of your important usernames and passwords, online accounts, and digital property. Photos can be one of the most sought-after digital properties after death. Specify what you want to be done with each item on your list if you become incapacitated or after you die. Keep your list updated and stored in a secure location. Redundancy is important. An Estate Planning attorney can help you update your will, power of attorney, and trust to address digital property. However, leave your passwords out of any such documents, as they will not be secure. Instead, there are several apps to keep passwords. Then, you just must ensure access to your phone and apps.

ADVANCED MEDICAL DIRECTIVE

An Advance Medical Directive, also known as a Living Will, Advance Directive, or Medical Directive, is a legal document. In this document, a person specifies what actions or decisions should be taken regarding his or her health if unable to communicate. This document will direct those in the medical community regarding such decisions as tube feeding, resuscitation, and the ability to "pull the plug." You select beforehand to accept or refuse medical care.

A Living Will, or an Advanced Medical Directive, is not a health-care power of attorney, which is discussed later. Both documents are important and should be in your Drop Dead File.

General forms are available for most states online. An individual's Advanced Directive can be reviewed or drawn up by your elder law attorney to capture specific concerns. This will provide the clarity around your decisions necessary for them to be carried out accordingly. Issues related to emergency treatment such as "Do Not Resuscitate" orders or an understanding of ongoing care like "Comfort Only" orders can be chosen and clearly decided. The directive can also cover other wishes such as tissue or organ donations.

Treatment options are often challenging and sometimes moral decisions for a family in crisis. When you give direction to such important decisions, your family can be clear and confident to follow your wishes. We encourage you to carefully consider whom to entrust for such difficult decisions.

DURABLE POWER OF ATTRNEY

Power of Attorneys can be difficult and confusing documents.

First, nobody likes to lose control. Second, a Power of Attorney can be difficult to execute. States can vary on governance. Financial institutions can vary in requirements. Plus, wording and the range of rights or responsibilities accorded to this role add to the potential confusion.

We will start by discussing both classifications related to a Power of Attorney: Financial and physical.

- **A Financial Power of Attorney** is a simple, and reliable way to arrange for someone to manage your finances on your behalf, from a single decision to the full range of financial decisions.

- **A Medical Power of Attorney** names someone whom you trust to act as your agent concerning medical decisions and care if you are unable to speak for yourself.

If you want to choose one person to speak for you on healthcare matters, and someone else to make financial decisions, you can do separate financial and healthcare Powers of Attorney.

Most estate or elder care attorneys will draw up a Durable Power of Attorney. This means that the person or persons you have chosen as your agent will retain their role, and the document will continue to be in effect should you become incapacitated and unable to make decisions on your own. Be careful of downloading simple Power of Attorneys from the internet, as they may or may not serve your purposes.

Healthcare and financial Power of Attorneys provide privacy and management divisions. You may elect to have the same people, or agents, selected for both documents. Or you may select different people for each area. You can select more than one person, typically in rank order, as an agent. If you select different people, please keep in mind the importance of collaboration and unity through the decision-making process. A family member need not be selected as your agent. You want to select the best person for the responsibility. Sometimes, this can be a family friend with medical or financial expertise. If there is significant conflict among family members, an appointment of an agent outside the family is recommended.

As stated early in the prologue, many Americans do not plan for end-of-life in any manner. Good intentions, although communicated verbally, are not sufficient unless formalized in legal documents. "Capacity" is the measuring rod for implementation of a Power of Attorney. If there is no legal plan in place for providing your agent with the power to make decisions on your behalf before there is a diagnosis of capacity, it will be too late. This sets off a domino effect of legal action which typically leads to a guardianship and conservatorship. These are very expensive and time consuming actions.

The right to make decisions does not naturally fall to the spouse in the moment of crisis. Unless your wife, or your husband has assigned you as a Power of Attorney, you will need to go through the often expensive and lengthy legal process of being assigned as conservator or guardian for your spouse.

One final addendum to the issue of Powers of Attorney. Often banks or other financial institutions require their own documents in relation to capacity issues or the passing of account holders. Similarly, the Veteran's Administration also requires working through a separate process. You may need to review all investments to assure legal right to access information and accounts.

POLST (Physician's Orders for Life Sustaining Treatment)

The "Physician's Order for Life Sustaining Treatment"[2] is just that, your doctor's order regarding your medical care as it reflects your wishes pertaining to end-of-life decisions. There are times you may need emergency care outside of a hospital, which may require what you might define as "extreme measures." In an emergency, the responders to your home or living community will begin to follow a list of protocols. Unless they see a POLST, they will follow their protocols regardless of your wishes if you are not able to respond.

You can get a POLST form from your doctor or hospital. This form is unique, in that, it must be signed by your physician (his care orders). The bright red POLST should be placed in a highly visible space for first responders. The POLST does not replace the Advanced Directive, but works in harmony, adding a more specific layer of direction for older or terminal individuals. There is some form of the POLST in 47 states. The name may be slightly different from state to state. If your state offers such a document, you can secure it from your physician.

HIPPA

The HIPAA (Health Insurance Portability and Accountability

---

[2] Survey Says People Have Too Many Passwords. Bruce Snell, Buzzfeed Tech, May 2016

Act of 1996) Privacy Rule[3], is a federal law, that gives you rights over your health information and sets rules and limits on who can review and receive your health information. The Privacy Rule applies to all forms of individuals' protected health information, whether electronic, written, or oral. The Security Rule is a Federal law that requires security for health information in electronic form. You will need to release this information for family and friends to speak with the medical community. Prior planning is essential for communication during a crisis.

FINAL WISHES

When a loved one has passed, the clock speeds up and slows down at the same time. It slows down because emotions are high as family members and spouses mourn and grieve the one they've lost. The clock speeds up as well because during the next few days to a week, a myriad of decisions come at the family members. Lack of planning causes undue expense and can add significantly to the challenge of the process. Remember, only a few decisions related to disposition of the body are necessary immediately. You will need to decide about ground burial versus cremation services, casket or cremation vessels. You also must decide funeral or celebration of life, flowers, programs, and the list goes on. Be aware that many decisions and actions regarding finances and real estate as well as the process of probate will require copies of the death certificate.

Make sure you get a minimum of five certified copies.

Pre-planning one's funeral is wise on several levels. First, pre-planning and pre-funding one's funeral and burial costs is a good investment. Second, funeral costs can soar when decisions are made during crisis and a time of grief. This can become a financial burden on spouses or family members who are left behind. Third, pre-planning allows for some creative thinking and cost-saving measures. Pre-planning alleviates the stress and burden of these decisions by your loved ones.

A lesser known, but growing choice, are companies who specialize in whole-body donation. The donated body will be used for research. Once completed, the body is cremated, and the remains returned to the family. Generally, all costs associated to transportation and cremation are covered by the company. However, it is important to note that some companies do not cover these costs.

---

[3] "Health Information Privacy," U.S. Department of Health and Human Services, last modified March 27, 2015, http://www.hhs.gov/hipaa.

Also, you can save on costs by searching online for available burial plots in nearly any cemetery in your area. People move, get divorced or remarried, and pre-purchased funeral plots become available often at a 50% or more savings over purchasing outright from the funeral company or cemetery.

Another challenging process for those left behind can be deciding how to memorialize their loved one. Be clear about what your preferences are regarding a funeral or a memorial. If you choose a more traditional service, write down your choices for music, pictures, obituary, and headstone. If these decisions are important to you, the family knowing they honored you is the first step towards dealing with their loss. If your loved one is a veteran, there are options available to you through the memorial cemetery which can be very honoring and helpful to the family.

The Decision Tree Plan is about planning AND communicating decisions. Remember, you are giving your loved ones a tremendous gift through the planning, allowing them to grieve your passing instead of the burden of managing your death. You give your children the ability to honor you.

Chapter Eleven
ROOT FOUR: SUPPORT PLANS

**Alone we can do so little, together we can do so much .
- Hellen Keller**

We all know the saying, "It takes a village to raise a child." The same could be said for a senior. We, the authors, were surprised by the number of caring professionals available to help seniors and their families through the aging process. We regularly speak with others who are totally unaware of the resources available. Many feel alone and overwhelmed. Building support teams of professionals, family, and community is essential. Whether it is for their expertise or the emotional support they afford us: individuals and groups in our lives play a big part in helping us achieve our goals and live out our choices. In this section, we will look at the teams that help provide this support.

PROFESSIONAL TEAM

As we age, we may experience any number of physical issues, and our care may be dependent on a group of varied individuals and practices. The goal is a team that advocates for your physical, mental, and legal well-being. This list can depend on the type or level of care you require. Your personal wishes regarding staying in the home or moving into a senior care community will direct your professional team members. Some providers will follow you, and eventually your trustees or executors, through the execution of your last wishes.

Physician. Most of us have a general or family physician. As you age, you may graduate to a physician who specializes in seniors, but either way, your regular physician is a major player on your professional team due to the knowledge of your health history and care. Under this heading, you may have others with specialties who are also advocating for your health: geriatrician, neurologist, psychiatrist, etc.

Health Care Manager or Social Worker. When you have a medical crisis, you will be assigned a social worker or case manager typically by the hospital. In some cases, and with some care plans, a healthcare manager follows along with your care. Involvement with this person may be only for a short period as they assure your care through the crisis and recovery period. You may elect to hire a case manager who will advocate and assist you through the healthcare system.

Home Health Provider/Caregiver. If you choose to age at home, your support team should include home health or home-care providers. These are two different levels of care. Some providers may do both. Generally, a home-care provider helps with basic personal needs and care including reminders and assistance with preparing meals. A home health provider gives medical assistance with certain levels of care, such as administering medications or assistance with more substantial physical needs.

Senior Community RN/Caregiver. Senior assisted living communities provide a team of caregivers. Also provided is an RN, PA, or other healthcare professional. Regular "care-team meetings" will keep you and others you wish to be included, up to date on your level of care, increased needs, etc.

Financial Manager. A financial manager is a key part of your professional team if resources warrant it. You, and those entrusted to your care, must have sufficient information about finances to help make decisions. The financial manager plays a role in the Income Stream Root to access cash flow. Cash flow will often determine where you can stay, and for how long. As you reach different physical or cognitive milestones, changes may need to be made quickly in preparation for a level of care issue.

Elder Law Attorney. In most cases, seniors are dealing with a trust, which has been set up to fund living and care needs as well as protect assets for changes in the future. Decisions regarding trusts, wills, Powers of Attorney, trustees, and executors need to be reviewed periodically, updated, or changed to meet the need or your wishes. Please see the Wills and Estates Root for more information.

Other Professionals may be a part of your team as needed. If your family struggles with conflict, then a professional fiduciary may be a good option. The professional team is a critical part of the Decision Tree Plan.

FAMILY TEAM

Family can play a huge role in successfully aging according to our decisions. Whether you have chosen to age at home with the assistance of a family caregiver or to move into a community, your family can make a difference in your success. Their support, ability to work together, advocacy for your well-being, and your decisions become increasingly important with each level of care.

Picking family members and roles is vitally important. Some decisions will be far more difficult emotionally, some will be more financial, and some more medical. When the time comes, pick a family member who will be strong and respected by his or her siblings. You know your children best. Remember, if a child struggles with addiction, poor financial management, or other issues, a support role may be more appropriate.

COMMUNITY TEAM

You have lived a good life, made friends, and built relationships. There is no reason that as you age these relationships need to disappear. If anything, you need to draw on these relationships to build your support team. If you are in a situation where a family caregiver is providing care, this team can be invaluable. The community care team can provide needed support on many levels.

Friends. Friendships built over the years can provide emotional support and familiarity that are a must as we age. For a family caregiver, they can mean a few hours of normalcy or even a break for the day to work on their own needs and relationships.

Church/Pastor. If you are part of a church, you may have built in relationships with your church family and pastor to help support you through the transitions that come with aging. Help with getting to and from appointments, going to the pharmacy, and grocery shopping are mainstays of a healthy and loving church family. Again, a church, pastor, or members who serve cheerfully will be a huge help to family caregivers who are providing care.

Social/Fraternal Groups. Some people find strong and supporting relationships through quilting, books, military, and service clubs. Common interests and activities can help in your emotional and physical care so you do not abandon them for a more sedentary lifestyle.

Take an inventory of those who can become part of your support team, both family and friends. Also, consider your present as well as future needs. Now, begin to match your support team members with needs, remembering not to burn them out. Build the team that will truly support you, be real with you, and bring you joy in your waning days ahead.

Chapter Twelve
BRANCH ONE: HOW WILL YOU TRANSITION

Life is pleasant. Death is peaceful. It's the transition that's troublesome.
- Isaac Asimov

Transitions and change are never easy; people of all ages resist change. Change usually involves loss. For example, you are leaving behind not just a house, but often a lifestyle. You may have a big kitchen and house for all the kids to gather. You may have a garage to work on cars or do wood working. Those activities will no longer be possible, as well as dozens of others, if you transition to a smaller home or care-giving facility. For many, if the husband is still living, transitions away from the house can feel like more loss than gain. However, a wife may look forward to no cleaning or cooking, so for her, she can see some gains in the transition.

If you choose to age in place, there are still many transitions. You may have a garage, but cannot physically work on the cars. You may have a large kitchen, but have lost the joy of cooking. You might have a garden, but now pay a gardener to tend it. Physical and mental limitations create thresholds of change. The change is moving from independence to more dependence. That is a difficult transition for most of us!

There is a movement today toward tiny houses and smaller dwellings. That choice automatically forces transition, simplicity, and downsizing. However, most people will not choose a tiny house. Eventually, we downsize not by choice, but by necessity. The progression for my mom was condo to assisted living. It took me a few months to go through her things and prep the condo for sale. She took some clothes, a chair, her television, a few kitchen utensils, and some pictures. When I needed to move her to an adult foster home for greater care, she only took her clothes and a few pictures. My mom was not a hoarder. She had a three bedroom condo, not a huge house full of furniture and "stuff." Yet, the task of going through everything was time consuming while trying to manage several businesses. Family members who oversee caregiving are sandwiched between the needs of their aging parents, the needs of their own families, and work. Daunting!

When is the best time to begin transitioning? NOW! Every year try to eliminate more stuff, either with parents or yourself. I am convinced one of the most loving things you can do for your kids is getting rid of the "stuff." My dad recently remarried. He initially kept his condo after moving in with his wife. He then sold it and went through most of his things. I expressed my gratitude over and over again. I live a great distance from my dad, so I could not personally help. I promised both my parents to uphold their wishes and help them age in place for as long as possible. The dementia finally took a toll for my mom. My siblings and I felt good by honoring her wishes as long as possible without verging on neglect. Upon the release of this book, my dad still lives independently with his wife at age 88. He is slowing down, but maintaining an active lifestyle. He works out three times a week at the pool, helping his joints and cardiovascular system. My dad has transitioned from a home, to a condo, to now sharing space with his wife in a condo. The only things I need to worry about at this point are a few personal items and executing his will. His wife will get all his personal property. I can honor his wishes and focus on my grief instead of going through an entire household of things. Thanks, Dad!

As a staff, we deal with many "stuck" families. The father or mother, or both, do not wish to leave the residence, even though there are significant health, financial, and safety risks. As discussed in the other branches, there are various options of how and when to transition. Even if a parent stays in the home and a caregiver is hired or a family member moves in, this act alone is a major transition from independent to assisted living.

Here are a few suggestions for those who are "stuck. First, make a plan. What is the goal? If the goal is remaining in the home, then the motivation to go through the stuff can be low. If the goal is the transition to a community residence, then the motivation is high because the house is typically sold. If the goal is to transition to a care community, then a date is often set because the community will begin charging rent upon the agreed upon move-in date. The plan should include how to disperse things to the family, what to sell, and what to give away. Picking a charity meaningful to the parents can help with letting go. Their things are going to a good cause.

Next, offer to help. Many seniors feel stuck because the task seems overwhelming, both physically and emotionally, to sort through the stuff. If the parent is open to the assistance, simply set dates for sorting. Depending upon the health and stamina of the parent, a full day may be overwhelming. A good three to four hours of steady work can slowly make some dents. Take some moments to cherish memories and consider who in the family may want any memorabilia or furniture. A professional organizer can be a great partner in downsizing. If the children are too busy with work and family to take the time necessary to sort, a professional organizer is very helpful to the parent(s). The organizer will give counsel on what to sell if a family member does not speak up for the item. They will assist in donations to your favorite charity as well.

You might have a parent with hoarding tendencies. There are professionals who can assist with this special situation. A more detailed plan is necessary, along with the counsel of the professional to assist both the family and the parent in the process.

Remember, transition is constant. Do what you can now with what you've got.

Chapter Thirteen
BRANCH TWO: WHEN WILL YOU RECEIVE CARE?

Being entirely honest with oneself is a good exercise.
- Sigmund Freud

A reality of life is that you don't know when death or a major medical event will occur. However, there is a wealth of information, history, and stories that are helpful to avoid the pitfalls surrounding a crisis. The creation of a Decision Tree Plan can guide you through the challenges and when to consider transitions.

In most cases, the aging process is the movement from independent care to levels of dependent care. The levels of dependence often determine thresholds of transition. A good plan will have several predetermined thresholds. These can be directed by your Decision Tree Plan to age in place or within a community setting. One should prepare for the potential threshold of reaching a physical or cognitive level that aging in place becomes unrealistic.

As much as your family loves you, they simply may not be able to meet the tasks of some physical and mental challenges should they arise in the aging process. Statistically, the physical and emotional strain on family caregivers (especially spouses who give care) can be tremendous. A Stanford study cited 63% of caregivers for a loved one with Alzheimer's or dementia will pass before their loved one[1].

So how do you decide upon these thresholds or triggers? What are the defining factors for a move from independence to higher levels of care?

Higher level functions were developed on a scale called Instrumental Activities of Daily Living (IADL). You can find more detail about them in the appendix. This scale measures activities like shopping, managing finances or medications, meal preparation, driving or navigating public transit, phone usage, and housework/maintenance. A change in these more complex daily activities signals the movement from independence to dependence. Giving up driving is a BIG DEAL for many seniors and their families. No longer managing finances is a significant shift from independence. Even allowing someone else to clean the house can be difficult. These are daily activities, and when your parent can no longer perform them, begin serious discussions with family members about the aging process. You should have a predetermined threshold for when to give up the car keys or allow someone to conduct your personal or corporate business. The goal of this book is to prompt parents to make their own choices, instead of making others decide for them.

Have you or your parent experienced a physical event or process that is overly challenging? You can find in the appendix a list of the

---

[1] Med.Standford.edu, May 2002.

"Activities of Daily Living" or ADLs, which define the need of care. ADLs are the common benchmarks used within geriatrics and all care communities to measure the level of care required for a person. Many family care givers can assist with one or two diminished ADLs. When the care moves beyond this, such as physical transfers being required, the needs may quickly become a more significant issue.

Most ADLs are physical in nature. The other major challenge can be cognitive. Dementia, which includes Alzheimer's, affects a large number of the population. Cognitive decline can be one of the most challenging experiences of aging. Receiving a clear diagnosis is not always easy. A starting point of discovering baselines by utilizing cognitive assessments and a brain scan by a neurologist will often yield an informed diagnosis. Detailing cognitive thresholds can be difficult. Your loved one will develop many coping mechanisms which mask the decline. The spouse or family caregiver can often live in denial surrounding the severity of the decline. Thus, the need for creating necessary legal documents to protect your loved one.

Whether physical or cognitive, it is important to get a comprehensive evaluation with several opinions. Without knowing the destination to which you are traveling, you cannot adequately plan the process of how to get there. Refreshing and reviewing the Decision Tree Plan will continue to make the journey clear and less bumpy for you and those around you.

We have discussed transitions in branch one. As you consider the WHEN of care, there are other branches to consider. Aging brings physical challenges which can make parts of a former life impossible, including everything from careers to hobbies. Similarly, cognition issues can cause freedoms taken for granted to be a risk for a parent or others.

One should think through other thresholds as well: such as when it is time to give up hobbies, workshops, boats...and yes, the car. These are difficult, even painful things to work through. These thresholds can create conflict when the family sees a parent who is not only at risk of harming themselves, but also others. One parent willingly gave up her car keys when she realized that it wasn't just her life in danger, but she could hurt someone else. Another loving, gracious, and peaceful act is defining the threshold of driving and giving up the keys.

Think through for yourself what situation, behavior, or diagnosis will be the threshold for choosing to give up a freedom and communicate this to your loved ones.

Chapter Fourteen

BRANCH THREE: WHO SHOULD GIVE THE CARE?

Allow others to give you loving care. Receive without guilt or apologies.
- Doreen Virtue

Where you receive care has a great deal of influence on WHO will give the care. If you select a care community, levels of care can be included. The more care needed, the higher the monthly fee. You may start with an apartment in independent living, with a small amount of services: cleaning, laundry, and options to eat at the dining room. As care needs increase, you have the option of bringing in Home Care and/or Home Health Services, or move into the Assisted Living Community. Home Health Services are different from Home Care Services. Most Home Care Services offer limited to no medical support. If your loved one needs medical support, you may need a Rehabilitation Community or Home Medical Services.

There are many Continuous Care Communities that include independent, assisted, and memory care. The question of WHO gives the care is typically included when selecting a care community. If you need increased care with more of a personal and family touch, you might consider an adult foster home. An adult foster home can be a bridge between assisted care and skilled nursing.

If you select to age in place at home, there are typically three options: Home Care Services, hiring a personal caregiver, or a family member elects to give care. There are many home care services from national franchises to local companies. Compare prices, level of services, and read reviews. You may wish to consider the range of services to meet increased needs of your loved one. Home service providers select the staff, train them, and schedule for your convenience. The service provider takes on the headaches of staffing, scheduling, payroll, etc. Although the most expensive option, it is also the most convenient.

You might consider hiring your own caregiver. Sometimes a hired caregiver is also a family member. When hiring your own caregiver, you take on the responsibility of an employee. You will need a payroll company or take on the responsibility yourself. You will need to send in state and federal, as well as any local taxes. The upside of hiring a caregiver yourself is the potential of a great fit for your family. Your loved ones become accustomed to the same person daily. Please remember you will need a substitute caregiver for sick days, vacation, and respite. You can hire a substitute or family members can rotate to give help.

More than 34 million Americans provide care to an adult family member age 50 or greater[1]. Family caregivers are selected for econom-

---

1   Family Caregiver Alliance Caregiver Statistics: Demographics., National Center on Caregiving, 2016

ic, as well as personal reasons. The cost of a care community or home services may not fit into the budget of a family. Sometimes, the only option for care is a family member or Medicaid. Many families desire to care for a loved one for personal, not economic reasons. For centuries, cultures from around the world cared for their aging loved ones. You were born and died in the same home. The care for an aging parent can be both rewarding and challenging. Family caregiving is an enormous topic and need. Check out the Appendix for links to free support and assistance to family caregivers.

Those who are responsible for care can often feel more of a burden of time and energy than initially anticipated. They are surprised about the amount of time financial and medical details can steal away from other life priorities. Conflict can erupt in the family over finances or choices of care, sometimes even over the smallest of details. This can be exhausting. Navigating the maze of Social Security, Veterans Benefits, Medicare/Medicaid, insurances, and other institutions can make your head spin. The Decision Tree Plan includes resources on all these topics.

Chapter Fifteen

BRANCH FOUR: WHERE WILL YOU RECEIVE CARE?

The most important thing is to try and enjoy life because you never know when it will be gone.
- Joyce Tenneson

When one is independent, the options of where to live are endless. As one ages and requires more care, the choices are more limited and fall within a few categories. The level of care needed, coupled with financial resources, are the two deciding factors which dictate WHERE you receive care. In this section, we will look at the different housing options available to seniors.

AT HOME

The majority of seniors want to stay in their homes as they age. "I will die in this house" is a common sentiment of people as they look toward the future. When one is healthy and independent, this is a viable option. Even as one ages and needs a little help, there are a multitude of resources to help seniors stay in their homes longer and be independent. These services range in price depending on the level of care needed and may become cost prohibitive depending on the needs. There are adult day care centers and wrap around service providers popping up, meeting a niche need.

When a higher level of care is needed than can be provided for in the home, or the costs of staying in the home becomes too great, people usually move into a community setting. If financial resources are not available for the needs, some family members will choose to take care of their loved ones themselves. The danger in this scenario is the burnout of the family member who is doing the caregiving. (See Appendix for Family Caregiving).

IN COMMUNITY

Living in community has many different forms. We will specifically look at the following:

- Shared housing
- Independent Living and Retirement Developments
- Assisted Living
- Skilled Nursing
- Memory Care
- Adult Foster Homes

Continuing care communities incorporate independent, assisted, and memory care all on the same campus. Once one moves onto one of these campuses, they can transition to higher levels of care as needed. As an independent resident, many communities require a "buy in." This is like purchasing a residence and is considered an investment. Once the loved one passes, most of this money goes back to the estate. There are some advantages of this system. The more funds applied for purchase reduces the monthly cost of rent. If financial resources become depleted, then the community will draw from the initial investment. There are also communities that stand alone and only include one or two types of care.

Shared Housing. A growing trend among cash strapped seniors is the concept of shared housing. As home prices rise and income drops for seniors, shared housing becomes an attractive option. This is not a regulated field. People market rooms through a variety of websites to reduce cost and increase community to share housing costs and chores. Recently nonprofits and others have jumped into this field (See "Shared Housing" in the appendix). Sometimes friends will get together and buy a house, other times, people will rent a room in someone else's home. Communities like this that focus on seniors are emerging and becoming an option. While not actually sharing housing, communities are springing up where seniors are living in close proximity to share resources catered to their needs. Local and state agencies are partnering with these new "villages."

Independent Living and Retirement Developments. More and more seniors are being enticed to more and more luxurious retirement options. Who wouldn't want to hang out in these brand-new state of the art facilities with multiple restaurant options, swimming pools, workout rooms, saunas, roof top terraces with concierges who attend to your every need? Usually, the more amenities, the higher the price tag. For those with unlimited resources, this is a dream come true for socialites who are ready to indulge in all that is being offered. For those with more limited resources, independent living still provides for all your needs while giving you the luxury of being as independent as you would like. These apartments are usually equipped with full kitchens and baths, with options of eating one, two, or three meals each day in the dining hall or on site restaurant(s). These communities provide a multitude of activities, and parking for a car if one is still driving.

Assisted Living. Assisted living is just that, help with living life and whatever needs exist. Some people need help with bathing, others with dressing or getting in and out of bed. Whatever the need, these facilities are usually equipped to help. The costs increase with the level of care. While this is one of the more familiar choices for seniors, and therefore one of the most widely available, the cost can still be prohibitive for some. For those with very limited resources, review of the policies surrounding Medicaid is critical. Not all communities provide rooms for Medicaid clients.

Skilled Nursing. With hospitals releasing patients earlier and earlier, people are now usually released to a skilled nursing or rehabilitation facility. At one time, these were referred to as nursing homes. With the advent of Assisted Living Communities, these have evolved into skilled nursing communities to provide the highest level of care outside of a hospital. In a rehabilitation wing, physical therapy is one of the main services. Overall, the goal is returning patients home or to their previous residence. Rehabilitation facilities are for short term, specific needs. Under Medicare or most insurances, such stays have a limit. If a family member needs extended care due to medical needs, then a skilled nursing facility is chosen. This, along with memory care, are some of the most expensive options available for increased care.

Memory Care. Dementia, which is often Alzheimer's, is affecting an increased number of the population. Not all people with dementia will need a memory care community, but when aggression or wandering is exhibited, this option may become necessary. Most memory care units are self contained, and are either part of a larger community, or they can stand alone. Some communities, such as the Green House Project[1], are creating smaller living situations. They incorporate a couple of memory care individuals in a smaller home-like setting with other assisted living residents. Most stand-alone facilities are smaller, locked units where the residents have their own bedrooms, but eat together and have a communal living area.

Adult Foster Homes. Adult foster homes can specialize in different kinds of care. These homes are smaller, with a limited number of residents which usually results in a higher level of individual care. They are run as a home with the residents living life together. Some homes

---

1   "The Green House Project," last modified 2017, http://www.thegreenhouseproject.org.

include children of the host family and are as varied as families themselves. People who are homebodies, and just like to live quiet lives are attracted to this option. Generally, adult foster homes are more open to clients transitioning to Medicaid. Adult foster homes can sometimes offer a bridge between assisted living communities and skilled nursing. The owner of a foster home may be a nurse and can offer medical assistance not offered at the assisted living community. The reality of the sheer need for senior care resources has given rise to many adult foster care homes being tucked into local neighborhoods. Adult foster homes have county and state oversight, which should be reviewed when seeking this option.

OVERSIGHT AND ASSISTANCE

Each community setting mentioned has county and state oversight, and should display or make available their most recent reviews, complaints, and licensing information. As with any major decision, one should do their due diligence to assure the safety and well-being of their loved one who needs assistance.

Similarly, for those choosing to live at home and receive in-home care at any level, a little research will provide you with the information to make an informed decision about who you choose to come into the home to provide care and assistance.

Lastly, the time and work involved in finding the right community can be significant. There are agencies that can assist you to find the right setting or level of care for you or your loved one. A placement agency will look out for you and provide as much individualized support as needed. Placement staff are familiar with the local communities and can match your need with a community. Placement agencies generally do this work for free with fees covered by the community that is chosen. We personally recommend local placement agencies over national, online options.

Epilogue

A tale of two families: one family with chaos and conflict, the other with planning and peace.

Richard and Mary lived for the present with little thought to the end of life. Mary and her children paid the price and suffered the consequences of poor planning. The chaos left their children, Becky and Rex, at odds. Planning through the Decision Tree Plan could have prevented many of the challenges and kept their relationships strong.

James and Joy chose purposeful planning early as a couple and continued to update their plans through the transitions of life. Their children reaped the benefits of their parent's careful planning. They walked beside their parents in the last days, confident of making decisions which honored James and Joy.

Each one of us gets to make the same choice. How will you choose?

Appendix

EXAMPLES OF THE DECISION TREE PLAN

For George (84) and Erma (81)
This information and these people are fictional

ASSETS, INCOME, AND CASH FLOW ROOT

Monthly Income Sources

Pension	$1,700
Social Security	$1,200
Dividend Income From Stocks	$1,500
Interest Income From Investments	$3,000
Total Monthly Income	**$7,400**

Monthly Expenses

Housing (Mortgage or Rent)	$0
Maintenance	$200
House Cleaning and Yard	$300
Taxes (Property, Income, Personal)	$2,500
Utilities (Electric, Gas, Cable, Internet, Trash, etc)	$400
Food and Entertainment	$700
Phone (Landline and Cell)	$150
Auto (Gas, Maintenance, Payment, Taxes)	$300
Insurance (Long-Term Care, Auto, Property, Health, Life)	$800
Gifts and Christmas	$300
Travel	$600
Charitable Gifts	$200
Out of Pocket Health Costs	$500
Total Expenses	**$6,850**

Asset Distribution

Real Estate	$500,000
Stocks and Bonds	$300,000
Investments (Mutual Funds)	$500,000
Cash	$100,000
Total Assets	**$1,400,000**

WILL AND ESTATE ROOT

George and Erma established a trust and named Joe Jones as the successor trustee and personal representative. Power of Attorney for financial and health, Advanced Directive, HIPPAA release, and any other documents are uploaded to the cloud and can be accessed via the internet. The physical originals are located in the safe deposit box at the bank. These documents are also uploaded to the *Honor Your Parent* secure portal.

SUPPORT TEAMS ROOT

Professionals
    Physician
    Dr. Smith, Portland Clinic, 503-123-xxxx
    Attorney
    Doug Adams, Adams and Jones, 503-456-xxxx
    Financial Planner
    Kurt James, 503-789-xxxx
    CPA
    Erik Funks, 503-321-xxxx
    Broker
    Joe Plano, 503-654-xxxx
    Legacy Coach
    Mark Duhrkoop, 503-987-xxxx

Non-Professionals
    First Baptist Church
    Pastor George Sealy, 503-147-xxxx
    Keith and Emily Stat, 503-258-xxxx
    Neighbors
    Diane Hamel, 503-369-xxxx
    Tom and Linda Knopp, 503-741-xxxx
    Friends
    John and Patti Fischer, 503-852-xxxx
    Jim and Rachel Cummings, 503-963-xxxx

END OF LIFE ROOT (Brief Summary)

George and Erma do not wish to have any medical attempts to artificially support for extended life. Details are in the Advanced Medical Directive.

George and Erma have pre-arrangements for burial at Miller Funeral Home (papers are in the safe deposit box). This includes plots at the cemetary.

George and Erma have suggestions for their memorial services to be held at First Baptist Church. Documents are uploaded to the cloud.

Needed information for obituaries are uploaded to the cloud.

WHERE TO RECEIVE CARE BRANCH

First Priority: Age in place in their current residential home. See Transitions Branch for changes.

Second Priority: Rose Park Senior Living Center
The Woods Community Center

Third Priority: Adult Foster Care, with the ability to care for appropriate needs.

WHO WILL GIVE CARE BRANCH

First Priority: Spouse, with support of other family members, and a hired caregiver. Support for household cleaning and lawn maintenance.

Second Priority: If spouse or family members can no longer give care, then Assisted Living or Adult Foster Care options. See Transitions branch for more information.

WHEN WILL CARE BE GIVEN BRANCH

IADL
Phone: Assistance to TTL or voice activated cell phone.
Driving: When spouse and children determine safety issues.
Meals: When no longer capable of meal preparation or weight loss signals loss of self-nourishment.
Housekeeping: When spouse and children determine assistance is

helpful.
Laundry: When spouse and children determine assistance is helpful.
Medication: Evidence of improper dispensing of medications.
Finances: Evidence of missed payments and improper use of funds.

ADLs
Bathing: When no longer capable of bathing for safety reasons. In home health for assistance, if needed for husband.
Dressing: When assistance is needed on a regular basis for dressing. Spouse will assist.
Toileting: When no longer capable of using the toilet without assistance on a regular basis, this will require a level of assistance that may include moving to a care community.
Transferring: When no longer capable of transferring from bed to chair, the level of assistance required may include moving to a care community.
Continence: If partially incontient, assistance in the home. If needing a catheter, then the level of assistance required may include moving to a care community or home health.
Feeding: Home care may need to be engaged for assistance.

TRANSITIONS BRANCH

Immediately, the residential home shall begin the downsizing process. Within a year, all non-essential property will be sold, given to children, or given to charities.

Parents choose to stay in the residential home and make modifications as necessary to age in place. This includes assistance with housekeeping, landscaping, and if needed, in home help as detailed in the When We Will Receive Care Branch.

Parents prefer to hire in-home care when needed rather than use a family caregiver.

When ADLs reach the prescribed level, then a move to a care community shall be carried out.

DROP DEAD FILE CHECKLIST

Remember to include **where** the documents and information can be located.

Legal Documents
- Will or Trust
- Durable Power of Attorney (financial and health)
- Advanced Medical Directive (living well)
- POLST or DNR (if needed)
- HIPAA
- Veterans' benefits need a separate Power of Attorney

Financial Documents
- Banking
- Investents (mutual funds, stocks, bonds, collections)
- Retirement (IRAs, Pensions, 401(k), Social Security)
- Personal Notes
- Debt
- Name of Financial Advisor

Deeds and Titles
- Real Estate
- Time shares
- Titles to vehicles, anything with a VIN

Insurance
- Agent contact information
- Auto insurance
- Life insurance
- Liability insurance (umbrella policy)
- Homeowner's insurance
- Health insurance
- Long-Term Care insurance

Taxes
- Tax records
- Expected returns or liability
- Contact information of tax professional

End of Life
- Prepaid funeral arrangements
- Cemetery plot
- Instructions about the body
- Instructions for funeral or memorial service, if any
- Obituary information
- Call list of those to notify
- Estimated number of death certificates
- Notify employer, Social Security, Pension plans, etc.
- Instructions for pets
- How personal property will be dispersed, and to whom (Will or Trust)

Online Accounts and Digital Property:
- Accounts, including social media with instructions
- Usernames
- Passwords

EXAMPLE OF DROP DEAD FILE BY AGE PROGRESSION

For James and Joy

JAMES AS A COLLEGE STUDENT. He kept these documents at his parent's home in a lock box.

Legal Documents
- Will (simple instructions about his body and personal property)
- Durable Power of Attorney
- Advanced Medical Directive
- HIPAA

Financial Documents
- Banking - Basic checking and savings. Bank and account numbers.
- Retirement - James started a traditional IRA. Included is where to find the statement of the account.
- Debt - Life insurance with parents as beneficiaries to pay off student loans and compensate for their help.

Deeds and Titles
- Where to find the title of his car.

Insurance
- Agent contact information
- Auto insurance
- Life insurance - parent's listed as beneficiaries
- Health insurance

Taxes
- Last return in lock box
- Current employment address and phone

End of Life
- Instructions about the body - he desires cremation.
- Instructions for his memorial service.
- He wants some of his personal property to be given to family and friends, and the rest to charity.

Online Accounts and Digital Property
- Uses a password app. Login information in the lockbox for all passwords for online platforms and accounts.

JAMES WHEN HE FIRST MARRIED JOY. These are instructions for BOTH of them. They placed all these documents in a safe deposit box at their local bank. The key to the safe deposit box can be found in their home office desk.

Legal Documents
- Will (instructions to each other and a named personal representative)
- Durable Power of Attorney
- Advanced Medical Directive
- HIPAA

Financial Documents
- Banking (name of bank and account numbers)
- Retirement - James and Joy each have a traditional IRA. There is a new 401k for James and PERS for Joy.
- Debt - James and Joy each know about their respective student loans. Student loan documents are in the safe deposit box at the bank.

Deeds and Titles
- Real Estate - Record of the financial transaction to purchase their first home.
- Titles to autos - They are both on the titles. Titles in the safe deposit box.

Insurance
- Agent contact information
- Auto insurance
- Life insurance - James and Joy listed in first position, parents in second.
- Homeowner's insurance
- Death insurance information

Taxes
- Where to find the file for tax records - home office file cabinet, lower drawer.
- Tax professional from last filing
- Expected refund or liability

End of Life
- Instructions about their bodies - cremation
- Instructions for the memorial service
- Obituary information
- Call list of those to notify
- Death certificates - estimated 4 needed
- Notify employer - check on any unused vacation or life insurance
- Nofity Social Security
- Will directs personal property to family and friends

Online Accounts and Digital Property
- No digital property at this time

JAMES AND JOY NOW THAT THEY HAVE CHILDREN. Kept in the safe deposit box at the local bank.

Legal Documents
- Will that directs the establishment of a trust upon death for the children. Guardians are named in the Will.
- Durable Power of Attorney
- Advanced Medical Directive
- HIPAA

Financial Documents
- Banking
- Investents - mutual fund account
- Retirement - Traditional IRAs, 401k for James, PERS for Joy
- Debt - Student loans are paid, credit cards are paid off each month
- Contact informaton for their financial advisor

Deeds and Titles
- Real Estate - kept only a few documents from the purchase of the home.

- Joint titles on their vehicles

Insurance
- Agent contact information
- Auto insurance
- Life insurance - listed each other as beneficiaries. Now direct death benefits toward the estate to set up a trust in the event of both parents.
- Homeowner's insurance
- Health insurance

Taxes
- Tax records - found in the home office.
- Expected returns or liability
- Contact information of tax professional

End of Life
- Instructions about the bodies - cremation.
- Instructions for the memorial service
- Call list of those to notify
- Death certificates - 4 needed
- Notify employer and check for any unpaid leave and life insurance.
- Notify Social Security, PERS, 401k and IRA financial institutions.
- Instructions for pets - James and Joy have a friend who will take the dog.
- The Will directs how to disperse their personal property. The guardians will recieve most of it. A few items go to other family members and friends.

Online Accounts and Digital Property
- No digital accounts.

JAMES AND JOY AT AGE 60. Important physical papers are kept in the safe deposit box at the local bank, some papers are digital, and some are located at the home office. The summary is kept in the home office file drawer.

Legal Documents (kept in a safe deposit box with copies in home office)
- Trust established with many details and titles of home, vehicles, etc. in the trust.
- Business documents - Operational Agreement and Buy/Sell.
- Durable Power of Attorney
- Advanced Medical Directive
- HIPAA

Financial Documents (kept in the home office)
- Banking - most reoccurring bills are automatically deducted from the bank account
- Investments - portfolio printed out annually with contact information of financial advisor/broker. All investments are checked annually for listed beneficiaries.
- Retirement - plans for when and how to begin collecting Social Security, draw on IRAs, 401k, and PERS. Plan was compiled by Financial Advisor.
- Debt - pay off credit cards each month. Statements are kept in the home office, in the lower file drawer in the file cabinet.

Deeds and Titles (kept in the safe deposit box)
- Real Estate
- Time shares
- Titles to vehicles, boat, jet skis, motorcycles, and snow mobiles.

Insurance (kept in the home office)
- Agent contact information
- Auto insurance
- Life insurance until age 80
- Liability insurance - umbrella policy was added when the business started
- Homeowner's insurance
- Health insurance
- Long-Term Care insurance

Taxes (kept in the home office)
- Tax records
- Expected returns or liability

- Contact information of tax professional. The professional handles business and personal taxes.

End of Life (kept in the home office or as directed)
- Prepaid funeral arrangements in the safety deposit box. Copy in the home office.
- Instructions about the bodies - cremation with direction of how to disperse the ashes.
- Instructions for memorial service, including location and order of service.
- Obituary information in the file drawer.
- Call list of those to notify
- Death certificates - 6 needed
- Notify employer or business partner agreement
- Social Security, PERS, IRA, or 401k financial institutions
- Instructions for pets - Jay will take the dog
- Detailed instructions in the Will for personal property to the children and others.
- All documents also scanned and stored in cloud storage

Online Accounts and Digital Property
- Accounts, including social media, with instructions - Facebook, LinkedIn, and Twitter instructions
- Password keeper that has all digital accounts with usernames and passwords.

EXAMPLES OF AN OBITUARY

This is a sample of information often used in obituaries. You may wish to use a more abbreviated list of information.

James Dean Smith died on October 15th, 2016, at 65 years old. He was born on July 20th, 1951 in Corvallis, OR. James graduated from Oregon State University with a mechanical engineering degree. After working for several engineering firms throughout the years, he pursued his real passion, fast cars! He opened Smith Speed Shop and later his son, Jay, joined him in the business. There was always a broad smile on James' face when he took a car out for a test drive.

James married Joy Warren on June 3, 1973. He is survived by his wife, son Jay Smith, daughter Jillian North, and son Jared Smith, along with five grandchildren. A memorial service shall be held at The Journey With Christ Church located in Beaverton, Oregon, at 7:00 p.m. on October 19th, 2022. Donations may be given to The Journey With Christ Church of a charity of choice.

Obituary Checklist
- Name of the person who died
- Date and location of death
- Age at death
- Date and location of birth
- Early education
- Marriage information
- Professional information, professional interests, and achievements
- Personal interests and personal characteristics
- Awards received
- Names of surviving family members
- Funeral service details, including the name of the funeral home
- Charity donation information

ASSESSMENT TOOLS FOR NEED OF CARE

These are functional assessment tools that can give insight into the need for care and help with understanding the cost one can expect for care.

The Lawton-Brody[1]. IADLs, or Instrumental Activites of Daily Living, are good guides to awareness of possible transitions and growing challenges in the aging process. The focus is activites necessary for living independently, such as telephone use, shopping, food preparation, housekeeping, laundry, transporting oneself, taking medication properly, and handling finances.

The Lawton-Brody Assessment and scoring process is widly available on the internet and easy to use.

The Katz Index[2] of Activites of Daily Living (ADLs) is used by care communities and other providers to assess the proper level of care needed by an individual. Most communities start with a base price for room and board. The actual cost of residency and care will be linked to the level of dependence one has based on their needs, as determined by the ADLs. Areas of bathing, dressing, medicine management, feeding oneself, mobility from bed or chair, and toileting or continence, are rated on a point basis in order to determine the cost for individualized care.

Similarly, you can find the Katz Index widely available on the internet.

COGNITIVE SCREENING

Please remember that these exams are used for screening only. If you suspect you or your loved one may have dementia or cognitive problems, please see your physician or neurologist immediately. Most of these exams should be administered by a health professional.

SLUMS was created by the Director of Geriatric Medicine at Saint Louis University. You can find this exam by going to:
                familymed.uthcsa.edu/geriatricts/tools/SLUMS.pdf

---

1   Lawton, M.P., & Brody, E.M. (1969). Assessment of older people: Self-maintaining and instrumental activities of daily living. The Gerontologist, 9(3), 179-186.
2   Katz S., Down, TD, Cash, HR, et al. (1970) progress in the development of the index of ADL. Gerontologist 10:20-30.

The **Mini Mental Status Exam (MMSE)**, also know as the Folstein Test, was developed in 1975. The MMSE is widely used and only takes 5-10 minutes, but is administered by a trained clinician. The test measures orientation, retention, attention, recall, and language.

Test Your Memory (TYM) can be self-administered or used by health professionals. The exam was developed by medical researchers at Addenbrooke's Hospital in Britain. The credibility of the exam is still being validated. Research articles published in the British Medical Journal show promise for the exam.

The Montreal Cognitive Assessment (MoCA) was created in 1996 by Ziad Nasreddine in Montreal, Quebec. Studies have demonstrated the MoCA may have greater sensitivity to detecting Mild Cognitive Impairment and Early Alzheimer's disease compared to the MMSE.

COST OF AGING IN HOME VERSUS CARE COMMUNITY

Asset Distribution

Expense	In Home Cost/Month	Care Community Cost/Month
Rent or house payment		
Taxes		
Electricity/gas bill		
Water/sewer		
Phone		
Garbage		
Cable/internet		
Upgrades for safe access		
Maintenance		
Condo/HOA fees		
Seasonal yard maintenance		
Security system		
Financial management services		
Daily money management services		
Payroll services		
Car payment		
Car maintenance		
Paid transportation		
Food expenses		
Meal preparation		
Cost of medicine		
Someone to oversee medications		
Housekeeper		
Care provider for personal care		
Medical in-home care		
Monitoring service		

Respite care		
Auto insurance		
Homeowner's or rental insurance		
Health insurance		
Long-term care insurance		
Total Expenses		

HEALTH INSURANCE FOR SENIORS OVER 65

Tips For Health Insurance
- **You can elect Medicare.** Medicare is available for those with work history of at least 40 credits. You need to select some form of supplemental insurance to combine with Medicare. Medicare is not automatic nor mandatory.
- **You may need to apply for Medicaid.** If you have less than 40 credits, then you will need to apply.
- **Speak with a Health Insurance Broker.** The broker will have knowledge and experience with the Medicare system and help you select the best options. The Medicare system can seem complicated and selecting the best option is very important. If you move from an Advantage to a Supplemental policy, you must pass through underwriting and may or may not be approved.
- **Have a timeline.** Three to six months from your 65th birthday you should choose your health plan (Medicare Advantage, Medicare Supplement, Part D - Drug Coverage) and choose your care team (primary care, specialists, dentist, optometrist, etc.).

WHAT TO DO WHEN SOMEONE DIES

As Soon As Possible
- Get a legal pronouncement of death. If hospice is involved, they usually handle the pronouncement. If not, you will need to call the police. They will need to conduct a brief investigation.
- Arrange for organ donation, if applicable
- Notify close friends or family. Ask the parent or loved one ahead of time to give you a list with names and phone numbers, if possible.
- Decide what to do with your loved one's body and arrange transportation - call a funeral home, cremation provider, or a full-body donation organization
- Arrange care for any pets and dependents
- If the person was living alone, seure the home or apartment and make a list of people who will have a key. If there are any other real properties, secure them as well. You may need to change locks or pins for an electronic door lock.
- Notify the person's employer if applicable

Within The Next Few Days
- Decide on funeral plans or celebrations
- Order a casket or urn, if applicable
- Ask the post office to forward mail
- Perform amore thorough check of the person's home, especially if you need to locate important documents
- Create a memorial website
- Write an obituary if the loved one has not already helped you write one

Leading Up To the Funeral Memorial Service or Celebration of Life
- Determine if you'll need financial assistance
- Look into veterans' benefits
- Choose funeral attendees
- Set the funeral or celebration of life schedule
- Order printed materials and flowers
- Coordinate food and drinks, if desired
- Spread the word using email, the local paper, and social media

Within The Next Few Weeks

- Order a headstone or plaque, if applicable
- Order several copies of the death certificate (usually six will do). The funeral home can normally assist you.
- Start the probate process with the will or contact your estate attorney. The Personal Representative will need to open an estate account at the bank.
- Contact the Social Security office. The funeral hoe will often contact them on your behalf.
- Notify any banks or mortgage companies. You will need death certificates for all financial institutions. You need to contact them if there will be financial hardships in meeting payments.
- Reach out to any financial advisors or brokers
- Contact a tax accountant
- Notify life insurance companies. They will need death certificates. Expect it to take 2-6 months to process.
- Cancel insurance policies
- Determine any employment benefits from the employer. Only the Personal Representative can contact the employer. The employer will ask to see a copy of the will.
- Identify and pay important bills
- Close credit card accounts
- Notify credit reporting agencies
- Cancel the person's driver's license and voting registration
- Memorialize their social media accounts (Facebook)
- Close email accounts once it is no longer necessary to keep them open.

HELPFUL RESOURCES

Websites
Social Security - www.ssa.gov
Medicare - medicare.gov
Veterans Administration - va.gov
Alzeheimer's Association - alz.org

Books
"How To Care For Aging Parents" by Virginia Morris
"A Bittersweet Season: Caring For Our Aging Parents - And Ourselves" by Jane Gross
"The 36-Hour Day: A Family Guide To Caring For People With Alzheimer's Disease, Other Dementias, And Memory Loss" by Nancy L. Mace and Peter V. Rabins
"Coping With Your Difficult Older Parent: A Guide For Stressed-Out Children" by Grace Lebow

Podcasts
The Alzheimer's Moment
Aging Today - PDX

For other resources see **www.honoryourparent.com**.